THANKS,
PENNEYS

VALERIE LOFTUS

WITH ILLUSTRATIONS BY

CIARA KENNY

MERCIER PRESS

MERCIER PRESS

Cork

www.mercierpress.ie

Text © Valerie Loftus, 2018

Illustrations © Ciara Kenny, 2018

Valerie Loftus has asserted her right under the Copyright, Designs and Patents Act 1988, to be identified as the author of this Work.

Ciara Kenny has asserted her right under the Copyright, Designs and Patents Act 1988, to be identified as the illustrator of this Work.

ISBN: 978 1 78117 622 1

10 9 8 7 6 5 4 3 2 1

A CIP record for this title is available from the British Library.

Printed and bound in the EU.

CONTENTS

INTRODUCTION

There's a story that you've probably heard in many different guises from many different people – one person might say their cousin's wife heard it in Dungarvan; another will tell you it was overheard in a church in Ballinasloe. Whatever the set-up of the story, the meat of it is always the same. Here's how they usually tell it:

'So there was this woman who had just moved to Dungarvan/Ballinasloe/[insert town of your choice here] from Poland/Nigeria/Canada/[insert Penneys-less country of your choice here]. Every day she'd go to work and listen to her colleagues chatting away. One woman would compliment the other's outfit or bag, and the complimentee would reply "Thanks, Penneys!" One day, one of them brought the new lady a cup of tea, and she turned to her and smiled and said, "Thanks, Penneys!" She just assumed it was the Irish way of saying "Thank you".'

THANKS, PENNEYS

It's maybe a little patronising to the subject of the story (assuming that this person even exists), but, really, they're not far wrong: 'Thanks, Penneys!' has become an unquestionable part of the Irish vernacular.

First it was used almost as an expression of surprise, like 'Can you believe this lovely thing is from Penneys?' Then, as Penneys began to step up their game considerably in the fashion stakes, it became a kind of conspiratorial wink: 'Yep, it's from Penneys. But keep it quiet or they'll all have it.'

Sometimes, if you're feeling particularly pleased with your purchase, you might tack on the price too: 'Penneys, €4!' Some women enjoy embellishing it with a little 'hun'.

It's a well-used hashtag, popping up time and again on Twitter and Instagram next to an artfully arranged display of recent purchases. It's printed on magnets. Nowadays, 'Thanks, Penneys!' is an expression of joy: glee over a bargain spotted and delight in sharing that with someone else.

In this book I will attempt to put how

PENNEYS, €4 HUN!

Irish people feel about Penneys into words: the frustrations, the funny bits, but most of all the love. Because it *is* love. Penneys is your spouse of twenty years, who you bicker and squabble with sometimes, sure, but at the same time who you can't imagine your life without. Maybe you don't even realise that you feel any of these things (most people probably don't think too deeply about their relationship with a clothes shop), but I am sure you will find something to relate to within these pages.

NOT YOURS

First things first: it's 'Thanks, Penneys', not 'Thanks, Primark'. Never Primark. Not to Irish people, at least, unless you want everyone to take an extreme dislike to you. The two names have caused quite a bit of confusion over the years. Are Primark and Penneys the same thing? Why is it only called Penneys in Ireland? And which one came first? Let me clear up any uncertainties.

Penneys is an Irish company – it has been around since 1969, when the first store was opened on Dublin's Mary Street by founder Arthur Ryan. When the brand expanded to the UK in 1971, it took the name Primark there to avoid legal action from the US chain JC Penney, but it's obviously still called Penneys at home. As it should be.

The noble Irish history of Penneys has gotten a bit lost in the global takeover of the company, which is now more widely known as Primark. (They can't even get 'Primark' right, either. It's Pr-eye-mark, not Preemark. The Lord bless us and save us.) In May 2017 *Cosmopolitan* published an article on their website breathlessly informing readers that Primark is called something 'completely different' in Ireland. Gasp!

They wrote: 'Brace yourselves. For starters, Primark isn't even British. The company originates from Ireland, where it came from humble beginnings in Dublin … The Irish have steadfastly stuck with Penneys, and despite the fact that the company now has stores all over the world called Primark, they are proud to be the purveyors of the original name.'

Yes we are! And it couldn't be changed to Primark now, not even if Arthur Ryan himself decreed it so (sorry Arthur). It would (1) cause a public outcry the likes of which has never been seen before in this country (and that's saying some-thing), and (2) be

KING OF PENNEYS
- ARTHUR RYAN -

completely ignored, as happened with The Point and Lansdowne Road. The idea of calling it Primark, even in the UK, makes Irish people distinctly uncomfortable. Angry even. It's Penneys! As it was in the beginning, is now and ever shall be. They can't take that away from us.

So, with that bit of rampant patriotism over with, let's begin.

THE LINGERIE SECTION

It's fair to say that a good 80 per cent of any Penneys store is dedicated to women and their various accoutrements – at least one entire floor plus whatever bits of the homewares section we'd like to claim. So much of the shop is already a temple to womanhood, but the lingerie section still manages to be a bona fide feminine explosion. It is here that the most sacred and precious secrets of our lives are kept; it is an Ark of the Covenant full of nipple covers, bra extenders and control-top undies, if you will.

It's rare that you see a man there unescorted by a woman. Some-times unsuspecting men will bluster in, looking for the tills, like a *Father Ted*

episode come to life, and turn an unusual shade of puce once confronted with floor-to-ceiling bras. Bras *everywhere*. Padded bras, bralets, sexy bras, ugly flesh-coloured bras. Just. So. Many. Bras. You can hardly blame them for being overwhelmed. We barely know where to begin ourselves.

But the lacy knickers and push-up bras are just superficial things, really. The important stuff is black or flesh-coloured, stretchy and decidedly unsexy. The lingerie section is often the place to find the final piece of a sartorial puzzle – those sticky strapless bras for tricky backless dresses, for example. Or VPL-free knickers. Or, you know, the pants with chicken fillets in them that aim to give you a Kardashian-style bum. (They were sold in Penneys once upon a time, and, hey, I won't judge if you decided to partake.) Slips, Spanx, 'body-shaping' vests, shorts that whittle down your thighs – these are the tools with which we create a woman. If it sounds vaguely torturous, well … it is. Nobody said the lingerie section was all saucy fun and games.

And the knickers. Oh, the knickers. You could spend hours rummaging through the piles of them, picking up and discarding countless pairs as you go on the often fruitless hunt for a size 10–12 in anything. Then it's on to the walls of bras that present problems all of their own, namely, 'My usual size is 34C, but what's my *Penneys* size?' and 'Is there anything here that won't be seen from Jupiter if worn under a white shirt?' This takes time and consideration. Cups are felt for padding (Too much? Not enough?), and the pros and cons of different knicker styles are weighed up, along with the likelihood that all these things will turn an unfetching shade of grey after one wash.

After all that, you inevitably land up at the till in front of a young male employee, who is forced to awkwardly disentangle and scan each item from the pile of lace and polyester you've deposited in front of him.

It's all a bit mortifying, but we always go back. When you're frantically in need of a strapless bra two hours before a wedding, the Penneys lingerie section is your only guaranteed option.

THE MAXIMISER

As much as we all love the filmy, support-free triangles of lace that make up fashionable bras these days, sometimes you're going to need them to do a little more than look cute. You want something heavy duty. This is where The Maximiser steps in. If that sounds like the name of a hefty, oiled-up WWE fighter to you, it's because it pretty much is – but instead of wrestling other hefty, oiled-up fighters, The Maximiser wrestles boobs.

Of all the sacred relics contained in the lingerie section's lost Ark, The Maximiser bra is probably the equivalent of the stone slabs of the Ten Commandments. Women utter its name with reverence. We probably should be petitioning the Vatican to have it canonised, seeing as it has performed more miracles for womankind than Mother Teresa.

But back to the boob-wrestling. The Maximiser is basically 99.9 per cent foam, and applying it to your person immediately pushes your bosom up to your chin, giving you the *look* of a buxom wench, no matter what size you actually may be.

It should not be deployed without careful planning, however, considering the boob-job rumours that it will inevitably spark amongst the uninitiated. (When one Kylie Jenner was photographed looking particularly busty, for example, many Irish women speculated that instead of going under the knife – as the media suggested – she'd gotten her hands on a Maximiser.)

The Maximiser is brought out for big nights out, weddings, Christmas parties … basically any time when you feel like you need WOW factor in the chest area. But with great power comes great responsibility – or, more accurately – a drawback or two, and so you're going to have to contend with both a restricted view of your own feet and the strange but inevitable sense of sorrow that comes with removing it and seeing your boobs for how they really are. Whether you can deal with this is up to you.

EIGHT TYPES OF PENNEYS KNICKERS EVERY WOMAN HAS ENCOUNTERED

Within the piles of pants in every Penneys store lie several key types of knickers. There are the ones that are literally too bad to even consider purchasing but which seem to be the only ones ever left in your size. Some you've actually bought, thinking they were grand, but then you wore them once and deeply regretted buying them and so buried them in a drawer until that terrible day when you realise that you've worn every other pair and have to make a terrible decision: turn a dirty pair inside out or wear the awful knickers. Truly it is Sophie's Choice. But that's just skimming the surface. Let's delve deep into the eight types of Penneys knickers that every Irish woman has encountered.

THE TACKY ONES

The tacky ones come in two flavours, so to speak. The first are screaming neon visible from the other side of the shop and are decorated with rhinestones and ribbons and leopard print. They mightn't be for you, but you can appreciate how confident they are. Like Jedward, but knickers.

The second flavour is more insidious. These ones are a nice, muted colour, with no spangles or frills apparent (except maybe a tasteful bit of lace). They look like grown-up-lady knickers for an elegant, grown-up lady like you. But then you turn them over and see that printed right across the bum in three-inch-high red lettering is something like 'NETFLIX AND CHILL'. Back to the drawing board, elegant, grown-up lady.

THE TACKY ONES THAT YOU SECRETLY LOVE AND ADORE

You are a Gryffindor and therefore you simply must have the Gryffindor knickers. You *must*. Oh, and these have Hello Kitty on the hip, look. Ah stop, how about these ones that say 'No Likey, No Lighty' like yer man from *Take Me Out*? Gas!

And, like that, €15 magically disappears from your bank account and the deep shame of being a grown woman with a drawer full of cartoonish knickers sets in. There's no choice left but to own it. Make it your 'thing'.

THE THONG-Y THINGIES

You know how every so often you see a cute thong (usually in a set with an equally if not more adorable bra) and say to yourself, 'Surely thongs aren't as bad as I remember?' That's how you ended up with approximately 124 of these things.

After a day spent trying to discreetly pick out an unpickoutable wedgie, however, you remember that, yes, thongs are exactly as bad as you remember. Until a year later, that is, when your memory has seemingly been wiped and the cycle begins anew.

THE 'SEXY' KNICKERS

You read an article in *Cosmopolitan* about how wearing lingerie is an act of self-care, and you knew at once that you wanted a piece of the action. 'Just for myself,' you think. 'Because I deserve to feel sexy.' And you do! Good girl yourself.

You could drop some serious coin in Agent Provocateur or La Perla, like the article suggests, but instead you throw a €14 Penneys set into your basket and feel on the cusp of something – a new life; a better, more confident you; a you who wears sheer mesh pants that have a keyhole over your bum crack for some reason. After two wears, however, they are relegated to the very bottom of the knicker pile (though sometimes you do bring them out for, er, special occasions).

THE PERIOD PIECES

These are sold in packs of five. They come up to your belly button. They are black or grey or who cares what colour because they serve a very distinct purpose, which is to carry you safely over the red tide like a sturdy, elasticated currach.

Sometimes you find yourself reaching for them even when Munster aren't playing at home. They just make you feel secure, somehow. And in today's world, who would begrudge a woman some of that? Even if it's coming in the form of huge-ass knickers.

THE 'JOKE' KNICKERS

These have something truly mortifying emblazoned on them – a picture of Ryan Gosling or Harry Styles, some Minions maybe – and were presented to you as a 'hilarious' Secret Santa gift by someone who surely doesn't know you from Adam. Why else would they think this was appropriate?

You shove the deeply unsexy articles right into the back of your knicker drawer, where you hope to never see them again. But then it's a day past what should have been laundry day and you're facing a dire knicker shortage when you spot Ryan/Harry/Minion staring at you from the murky depths. And you figure that, knowing your luck, this will probably be the day you get knocked down by a bus and the Guards find you in your Minion knickers. But you'll have to take the chance. Just this once.

THE SUCKY-INNY KNICKERS

They were once flesh-coloured but have gone bobbly and grey in the wash. They take you half an hour to get into and out of. You have a contingency plan in place on the off-chance you ever pull while wearing them. (It involves subtly peeling them off and stuffing them into your handbag. You're not sure if you'd actually get away with it. But it's important to have some sort of plan in place.) You're slightly mad about how much you value them, considering they're a tool of the patriarchy and all … But the figure they give you! They'll have to prise them out of your cold, dead hands.

THE ANCIENT ONES

It's a wonder they've lasted so long when so many nicer, more expensive ones have gone to Knicker Heaven before them. They've been dulled by years of washing and whatever design was on them originally has long since peeled off, leaving them looking vaguely dirty all the time. Still, you can't quit them. They've put in the work and you owe it to them to hang on to them until they actually have a hole in them. It's the least you can do.

TIGHTS

Tights are Penneys' MVP. Think of all the Penneys shopping sprees you have enjoyed over the years. Now think about how many of them have been initiated by your 'just going in for tights'. It's scary, isn't it? Living in the climate that we do, tights are so important to us, and nowhere is that more apparent than in the hosiery section of Penneys, where you can find more kinds of tights than you are ever likely to need in your lifetime.

Let's take a trip down memory lane to revisit some of the strains of Penneys tights we've all probably used and abused over the years, shall we?

TAN TIGHTS

Oh Lord, tan tights. There is not a woman in Ireland who has not worn these on a special occasion, thinking that they looked 'natural' when in actual fact you could see the shine coming off them from about two miles away. Does anyone other than Kate Middleton and flight attendants wear tan tights any more? Could they be extinct in a few years, what with fake tan taking over their main job? While I do not care for tan tights, I nevertheless respect their hustle. The day that we can't go into Penneys and buy a pair will be a sad day indeed.

THE 'BODYSHAPER' TIGHTS

These always seem like a great idea until you're trying to squeeeeeeeze yourself into the 'bodyshaping' part like a sausage into its casing. If you do manage it, you spend the rest of the evening feeling them slowly rolling down your belly, undoing all of your hard work. And when it's time to take them off? Well, you might as well cut them right off your body because you're never going to get back into them again. The joys of being a woman!

THE 10-DENIER ONES THAT COME IN A LITTLE BOX OF FIVE

You see them, and you're like, 'Ooh, so many tights for so little money!', but then you quickly discover that you have to mind them like little, delicate, easily ripped babies. First you must find a box

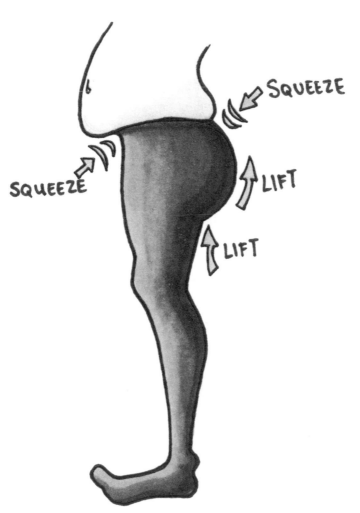

that no one else has opened and rifled through, which is a task and a half in itself. Once purchased and ready to use, you have to try and carefully roll them onto your legs without piercing them with a fingernail. And THEN you have to successfully wear them for a whole day or night without laddering them. This is a test I've yet to pass. I will never be an elegant sheer-stockings lady!

THE OCCASION TIGHTS

You know, the one with bones on them for Halloween or the glittery ones they do for Christmas (which I personally wish they sold all year round because CUTE). These are usually bought to go with some specific outfit or costume, after which you leave them to languish in the drawer, unable to wear them but afraid to throw them out because what if you suddenly need tights with bones on them again? WHAT IF???

SUCH SPORKLE ♡

MUCH FESTIVE ♡

FOOTLESS TIGHTS

Footless tights, to me, conjure up an image of teen discos, where they would be paired with a neon-coloured (or 'luminous' as we would call it) vest top, a ra-ra or denim miniskirt and a strand of plastic beads looped around the neck. Tell me you see this too?

OPAQUE TIGHTS IN A RAINBOW OF COLOURS

There was a time when wearing plain black tights was almost frowned upon. Sure why would you when you could wear cobalt blue or violet or red? I blame girl band *The Saturdays*, who based their whole 'look' around coloured tights and seemingly inspired many other gals to do the same. (Shame on you, Una Healy.) In 2009 there was no outfit I wouldn't wear purple tights with. It was *my* 'look'.

Nowadays, all I ever want is a black pair of tights in a size M, and all Penneys wants to give me is mustard and brown and navy. It must be some sort of karmic punishment.

DARINGLY PATTERNED TIGHTS

I'm talking about the ones that are so obtrusively patterned that they inevitably wind up in the reduced section because no sane person wants to go near them. Every picture from my second year of college is a reminder that I used to quite seriously wear sheer tights with big black stars all over them. I could have just worn plain sheer tights, but that wouldn't have been 'individual' enough for me. As you can see, my history with tights is a bit wild and reckless, and I honestly struggle with the decisions I made to this very day.

LITERAL 200-DENIER MONSTERS

Like, these should probably be classified as leggings. (Though somehow they're much less see-through than the actual Penneys leggings. But more on those later.) The 200-deniers are virtually indestructible, warm as hell, and some of them even come with built-in socks so you can wear them with boots. Even writing about them makes me feel sensible, despite the fact that I am usually the fool who insists on wearing 60-deniers all winter.

But here's the essential truth of Penneys tights: no matter what kind they are, they're here for a good time, not for a long time. Towards the end of their lifespan (it's not been officially confirmed how long that typically is, but for your average opaque pair it usually seems to be about six to eight wears and a couple of washes), the elastic starts to go and they betray you. Yes, what used to be perfectly stay-y upp-y tights become fally-downy tights – and when that happens, there's no coming back from it. This curse is not strictly limited to Penneys tights, of course, but since most of the female population would be scandalised at paying more than €4 for two pairs, we see it with them most often. If you've never experienced fally-downy tights before, you're either lying or extremely lucky. In which

SHHHH!

case – how is that? What secret magic tights are you buying that never start to peel away from your arse? Write to me and let me know, and save me from the hellish experience of ever wearing fally-downy tights again.

Let me try my best to describe the experience of wearing treacherous tights to you. With every step you take, they are slowly inching down your body, which, as you can imagine, is a most unpleasant sensation. This feeling can turn even the most confident woman into a self-conscious mess. No one knows it's happening except you, but still you start to wonder if the gusset has become visible beneath the hem of your skirt. It can't have, but MAYBE IT HAS? You spend the whole day stopping to give the tights an almighty hoick to get them back to where they're supposed to be. At first, you try to do the hoicking in private, but by the end of the day you're in the middle of the street clutching handfuls of your tights and heaving them up with all your might. There's just no time to be shy when it's either that or clawing the fecking things right off your skin. You'd think after all this we'd throw them straight in the bin, but something about them makes us give them a second chance.

When we do eventually throw them out, we have to go back to Penneys again for the tights expedition-cum-shopping spree, and the cycle of the fally-downy tights is perpetuated over and over again. Our endless need for black tights will surely be the end of us.

RAWR!

NEW JAMMIES NIGHT

There's something about getting new pyjamas that is just pleasure epitomised. You never go to Penneys specifically to buy them; they come to you, drifting into your eyeline through a sea of plastic make-up bags and leopard-print belts. It's like that moment in a rom-com when two potential lovers' eyes meet across a crowded room – time seems to stop, and everyone and everything else just fades away. All of a sudden, you know that the time has come to treat yourself to new pyjamas. The last time you checked, you thought your pyjama drawer was actually quite full, but now you see that you were quite wrong. There is a pyjama-shaped hole in your life and these ones fit right in it.

THANKS, PENNEYS

Your choice of pyjama dictates how the rest of the evening will play out. Sometimes it's a sophisticated satin set that catches your eye, as you want to play at being the type of fancy woman who spends money on silk pyjamas. Other times it's a pair of the softest, fluffiest pyjama bottoms that call to you, holding the promise of extremely cosy times ahead. Then some days you fall in love with a *Rugrats* nightdress that immediately transports you back to worshipping Angelica Pickles as a seven-year-old, and you feel like it'd be rude to your younger self to leave it behind.

As soon as the new jammies are chosen, purchased and safely on their way home in a paper carrier bag, everything else you have to do that day is irrelevant. All that matters now is preparing for, and enjoying, New Jammies Night. If you had a secretary, you'd tell him/her to clear your schedule. You simply must put them on ASAP – but not before making the necessary New Jammies Night preparations, of course.

First, it is important to get in the shower and wash all the dirt from your pre-new-pyjamas life from your body. You can't be taking any of that negativity into your New Jammies Night. If you're feeling particularly luxurious (and you're a lucky sod who has a nice tub in your house), you might have a bath. Being squeaky clean is a key element in the enjoyment of new pyjamas. Putting on fresh bedsheets is a great bonus too, but not essential.

Next, you must cleanse yourself spiritually – there can be no thoughts of work or the leaky dishwasher or that dose Sandra next door – not tonight. Tonight is a Sandra-free zone.

Once the pyjamas are on, you can go about the business of comfort. Your feet cannot be neglected, and fluffy socks or slippers must be applied to keep them toasty. Perhaps a hoodie or dressing gown can be added, if a little extra warmth is needed up top. As the intention is to move as little as possible for the rest of the evening (which is highly recommended on New Jammies Nights), a nest should be constructed on the couch or in the bed with a mass of pillows and blankets. Smelly candles are essential. A suitable film or TV show must be selected on Netflix, with an emphasis on the cosy and nostalgic (like a few episodes of the BBC *Pride and Prejudice* with Colin Firth, or any Tom Hanks/Meg Ryan film. Y'know. COSY). Or you might decide to read a book instead, depending on the vibe of the evening. Top New Jammies Night beverage choices include hot chocolate, tea or a glass of wine, and some sort of delicious snack is absolutely key. (Maybe you'll even get a takeaway? Treat yourself?) If you're particularly smug about your set-up, you may even Instagram a picture of your new jammie-clad legs, hand clutching your wine glass or mug, with hashtags like #snuglife or #socosyrightnow. That's right. Let 'em know. Let 'em aaaaaallll know.

Absolutely no one is allowed to question why you are behaving in such a manner on a Tuesday evening. Not your housemates, not your parents, not your partner. It's New Jammies Night, bitches! And this glorious occasion comes but a few times each year. (Or more if you seriously can't stop buying pyjamas. In which case, you might have a problem.)

If you don't appreciate the importance of it, that's your issue. Now move along. You're interrupting the cosy.

Stunstagram

♡ 💬 #SNUGLIFE<3

GRAND PENNEYS TRADITION #1: THE CHRISTMAS JAMMIES

At some point in the past decade or so, Irish people decided that you couldn't wake up on Christmas morning wearing old pyjamas. It'd be rude to the Baby Jesus, or Santa, or whichever family members you had staying on air mattresses in the living room. You couldn't have them seeing you in the old rags you usually snooze in, like. At Christmas time, everyone must look smart and on-theme – even while sleeping or vegging out in front of the TV, stuffing fistfuls of Roses into their gobs. And lo, unto us the Christmas pyjamas were born.

Christmas jammies are different to normal jammies. They are a bit more special and noble in purpose. Here are some important Christmas-jammie criteria that have been identified over the years:

1. They must have at least double the cosiness of a normal pair of pyjamas, which means they need to be fleecy, fluffy, or at least brushed cotton. You will likely wake up in the night sweating because of the heat of them, but that is entirely besides the point, which is MAXIMUM COSINESS AT ALL COSTS.

2. They must provide optimal comfort during waking hours, because even if you've carefully selected a Christmas Day outfit, you'll probably end up in your jammies again before long.

3. There must also be plenty of room to accommodate your food baby, or indeed food babies (because some of us will look like we're expecting twins after a good feed).

4. There must be some sort of festive element to them. At the very least, your pyjamas should feature a tasteful Fair Isle-style print – though, if we're being honest, that's kind of a cop-out. Like the Christmas jumper, a real pair of festive jammies should be a bit mortifying. If they don't have a big jolly snowman or the Coca-Cola truck or a

groanworthy pun-based slogan on them, you're not truly getting into the spirit of things.

5.   Matching fluffy socks, slippers or dressing gowns are optional extras. Onesies have also been embraced as Christmas jammies over the past few years, but whether you enjoy clambering out of them (and subsequently freezing your bum off) every time you have to go to the loo is down to personal preference.

Here's how obtaining your festive jammies usually goes down: on Christmas Eve you are permitted to open one present. This is always treated like it hasn't happened every year for as long as you can remember. 'Wow!' you think, exchanging a disbelieving glance with a family member. 'I can't believe we're getting away with this. This is UNPRECEDENTED (since last year).' You then sit in a state of great agitation as the gift is retrieved from under the tree and presented to you. You rip the wrapping paper off, saying something like, 'Ooh, I wonder what this could be …', while your mam insists that she couldn't possibly know, sure isn't it from Santy, what would she have to do with it? And then, sure as the sun rises in the east, there are the Penneys pyjamas, warm and soft. Like you would on any New Jammies Night, you hop into them as soon as is humanly possible and watch a bit of cosy Christmas telly before toddling off to bed, feeling as excited about the following day as you did as a child.

It's going to happen this year, and next year, and the year after that, and if you have kids you'll probably do the same thing for them. The pyjamas themselves may change, but the ritual stays reassuringly the same. And that's a bit of Christmas magic in itself.

THE LIFE OF A PENNEYS PAPER BAG

Hello. My name is Kevin, and I am a Penneys bag. 'Stop that. Penneys bags aren't sentient,' I hear you say. Well, there's a lot you don't know about my people. And we wouldn't expect you to, either, considering how you never even stop to think about us. Really! With everything we do for you.

Our lives are cold and hard. My first memories are of being packed with dozens of my brethren into a dark cubbyhole, sandwiched on top of one another. I remember the first time I saw that strip of light far above me, holding all the promise of

Hi! I'M KEVIN, THE PENNEYS BAG! :)

another, better world. And for a short while, I actually believed that it *did* lead to a better world. But then the terror started. A pair of black slack-clad legs strode in front of our cubbyhole, and the sound of muffled voices and beeps began to float down from the direction of the light. All of a sudden, a great hand loomed, grabbing at the topmost bag in the pile. He was drawn upwards, screaming in horror. He didn't understand. None of us did.

THANKS, PENNEYS

Whispers came up the pile from the older, more seasoned bags. They informed me that it was our duty to be used to house mysterious items such as 'cold-shoulder tops' and 'hair bobbles'. It sounded grand, but I wondered where we went once we were chosen. What happened to us afterwards? I was about to find out.

One day, my closest friend, Mabel (literally my closest friend: she sat right on top of me), was snatched away to her service. I wept for her, because I knew we would never see each other again. But I also wept for myself, as I knew that finally my time had come. I would learn what had happened to all of my brothers and sisters. Sure enough, moments later, the Great Hand reached down for me. 'Goodbye, friend,' I whispered to Terry, the bag below me, before the bright light blinded me.

I was wrenched open to accommodate the strange items I had heard so much about: a five-pack of black ankle socks, along with a can of dry shampoo, which I have to say hurt quite a bit. Can't you humans be a bit more gentle? But I suppose it's not in your nature. I know that now. Because, as I was grabbed by my new owner and taken through the shop, I saw things. Terrible things. I saw paper bags like me ripped right down at the handles by careless shoppers. I saw the sharp corner of a picture frame protruding through the face of an innocent young bag. 'I wish they would just kill me,' he called. 'Every moment I live is agony.' All I could do was watch.

Outside was no better. It was raining hard, and each drop hit me like a bullet. Right there in front of my eyes, a soaking wet bag succumbed to his injuries and burst open, contents spilling onto the ground in gruesome fashion. I wanted to vomit at the sight. But the woman who had claimed me? She protected me. She held me close to her chest to ensure I was not harmed by the raindrops. She placed me carefully on the back seat of her car where, exhausted from my ordeal, I allowed myself to sleep. That's how I ended up where I am now.

I am one of the lucky ones, I know. I have been sitting on a chair in the corner of a bedroom for some time now, the ankle socks and dry shampoo still stored inside me. The woman who carried me here seems to have completely forgotten about me – she keeps throwing items of clothing on top of the chair, concealing me from view. Soon she will no doubt feel guilty about the growing pile of clothes that keep me so safe and warm and hang them all up in her wardrobe again. Then I will be exposed and in real trouble.

There is no chance of me being used to carry her shoes to work. That job she reserves for the battered but still sturdy Victoria's Secret bag that sits just below me on the floor. His name is Chuck and he is from America, he tells me. New York City. The woman brought him all the way back to Ireland to use him for this very purpose, and he is very smug about it. I hate Chuck. But I'm stuck with him until the day I am finally discovered and sent to my final destination. Chuck says I will go out with the recycling, where I will be turned into something else. This doesn't

seem too bad to me. Maybe I will come back as a Brown Thomas bag, the big ones they use to transport designer handbags. I'd like that. I've always felt like I was meant for bigger things than hauling around socks and underwear.

For now I wait, and remember all of my

brothers and sisters who have been cruelly ripped from this world. Perhaps my story will inspire you to take pity on the Penneys bags in your life. We deserve more than to disintegrate and die on the rainy streets of Ireland or have your pointy purchases make holes in us.

Be kind. Take care. And think of little old Kevin.

CHRISTMAS IN PENNEYS

Nothing says 'Oh God, how is it November already?' like the familiar old debate striking up again. In one corner, you have the Scrooges complaining that Christmas gets earlier every year. ('Sure doesn't Brown Thomas open its Christmas shop in August, for God's sake, and why can't we just leave it until the last two weeks of December like it used to be? Ah, it's a disgrace, Joe!') In the other corner are the Buddy-from-*Elf* types who basically live for Christmas, and they want you to know all about it. They're the ones you see in your Spotify sidebar listening to Christmas songs in September, itching to put the decorations up as soon as the evenings get darker. Let's not get it twisted: both of these groups can be incredibly annoying. Relax, like. It's just Christmas.

The fight between the Scrooges and the Buddys means especially little to the people who are actually stationed in the festive trenches. I'm talking about the retail workers, without whom Christmas as we know it would cease to exist. For them, the whole

thing starts in late October, when the temporary staff slip quietly onto shop floors to commence preparations for the season. (So for what it's worth, Scrooges, you are correct. It does begin very early. This is not a licence to be even more insufferable, though.) Like many young Irish people, I did a season as a Penneys Christmas staff member, long, long ago. I was just excited to have a job. I'd worked retail at this time of year before, in a much smaller shop in a much smaller town, and thought I'd be well prepared for what lay ahead. But nothing can really prepare you for Christmas in Penneys.

It's smooth sailing for the first few weeks. The Christmas shop with its decorations springs up somewhere in the store, usually on the main shop floor, and you, of course, get the few remarks from customers about how early it does be getting. You also get the clever, organised people in to snap up a few of the nicer decorations and stocking fillers to put away until December. A few weeks pass, and you start to notice that people are actually buying the Christmas jumpers that have been sitting valiantly on the shop floor since September. Then you look up from folding T-shirts one Saturday afternoon at the beginning of December to see the place swarming with people. From then on, the place is never less than 80 per cent full during opening hours.

CHRISTMAS IN PENNEYS

The idea for *The Hunger Games* must have been born in a Penneys on a Saturday in December, such is the air of desperation and treachery. There are no allies here. It's every person for themselves. Then the first disaster hits: the shop is cleared right out of tinsel. My God, we have no tinsel! You have to tell people that there's no tinsel, and sorry, those lovely Mickey Mouse baubles they saw on Instagram have flown out the door too. No, you're sure there are none in the back – the back being a sprawling and mysterious warehouse that no one who works there can comprehend, as opposed to the neatly organised stockroom many people imagine. They don't understand, but how could they? You, personally, have ruined their Christmas, and there's nothing that can be done about it.

You're confronted with problems you've never even considered in the past, like how best to put three rolls of wrapping paper into a carrier bag without it splitting down the side. (Sorry Kevin!) You think about all the time you wasted studying algebra when you could instead have really used a class on counting change without it melting your brain. You're double-bagging like you've never double-bagged before. Your Christmas small talk is *impeccable* – 'Are you having many over? TWENTY-FIVE? I'm sure it'll be grand.' – but you're also well able to hold your tongue when a customer dares to complain about the place being busy. (Why did you come here on a Saturday in December then? Sorry. I've just always wanted to say that.) Thrice

you've heard a parent referring to you as 'the lady' who is going to inform Santa of their child's bad behaviour. As if you would grass on a kid like that. But unable to say anything you just have to let the child fear you.

None of this was in the job description! And it only gets worse as it draws closer to Christmas Eve. The panic in the air is tangible, and there are always at least two children screaming somewhere in the depths of the shop. People are

"EXCUSE ME!"
"WHERE IS THE WRAPPING PAPER?"
"HAVE YOU THIS IN A SIZE 14?"
AAARGH!!
PAUL
"IS THIS REDUCED?"

grabbing things that you sincerely hope they don't intend to give as gifts, like lint rollers and packs of the fancier-looking hangers. The simple act of trying to get to the staffroom for your break becomes a scene from *The Walking Dead*. The door is just in sight, deliverance *so* near, when a customer looms out of the shadows to ask if there are any elf onesies left. Just as you finish dealing with them and start for the door again, another person grabs you to see if, by any chance, there are any of those unicorn make-up brush sets in the back, please, they're desperate. *Just let me go, you monsters! Leave me to eat my sad sandwich in peace!* There are no elf onesies or unicorn brushes here, not on 23 December. You know this. You *have* to have known this.

There are a few saving graces, one being that Penneys shops fortunately, thankfully, *mercifully* have no piped music. At Christmas, this means you can go about your work without Bono roaring 'WELL TONIGHT THANK GOD IT'S THEM' in your general direction. Too many Christmas songs have been ruined for retail workers in this way, and you have to be grateful to Penneys for (somewhat inadvertently) taking a stance on the issue. You get enough of Bono roaring at you everywhere else.

Another perk is the camaraderie that develops between the workers after a few weeks of wrestling with hangers and being 'the

♪♪ DO THEY KNOW
IT'S CHRISTMAS
TIIIIME ... ♪♪

lady' to bold children. They're the only people in your life to whom you can bellow 'I HATE THOSE FECKING KNICKER TABLES' and not only will they understand, but they'll agree. They'll tell you their own story about a child with a particularly piercing scream, or the time they discovered a leaking McDonald's milkshake wedged behind the king-size duvet covers (which happens more than you know), and you'll feel better.

So when the festive period is over and it's time to go back to your normal life, you almost find it difficult to relate to anyone who *hasn't* worked in Penneys at Christmas time. How do you let them know that you've changed, that you've seen things that have made you question everything you thought you knew about the human race? It should be mandatory for every Irish person, old and young, to do at least a month's seasonal work in Penneys. I can't say for sure, but I have a feeling it'd sort us all out. Rudeness to retail workers would be completely eradicated. Christmas shopping crowds, and subsequently Christmas shopping stress, would be a thing of the past, because people would see at first hand the effect of last-minute-itis on our cities and towns. No one would receive a bad gift again. (Maybe. No promises here. Some people are just not natural gift-givers.) Taoiseach, are you listening? I'm ready to be consulted on this plan to radically overhaul Ireland for the better. Call me.

THE PENNEYS OBSTACLE COURSE

Right, you're on your way into Penneys and you have ONE THING to get. One thing. You're going to be in and out in two minutes. Just walk in, get the tanning mitt and leave. On your marks, get set aaaaand: GO!

1. Oh no! It's Going Out Top avenue. Walk through without stopping to check the price tag on anything. Try your best!

2. There's a staff member coming towards you, wheeling one of those death-trap clothes rails. Quick! Dodge it before you lose a limb!

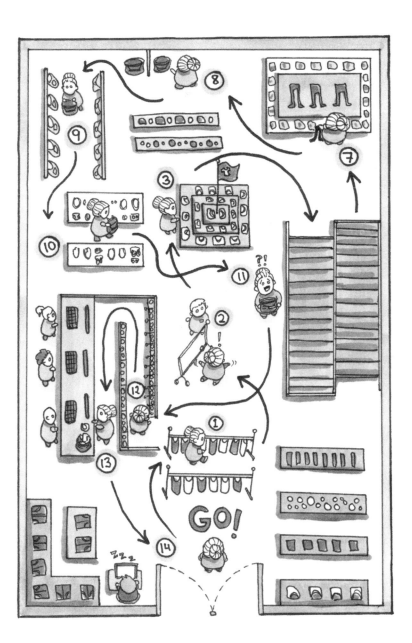

3. Okay, you've arrived at T-Shirt Mountain with all your appendages intact. Extract the plain white V-necked one in size 14 that you've suddenly decided you want from the pile, without disturbing any of the others.

4. You're passing the escalators now. Go up to Shoe Island for a look. But make it quick, for God's sake.

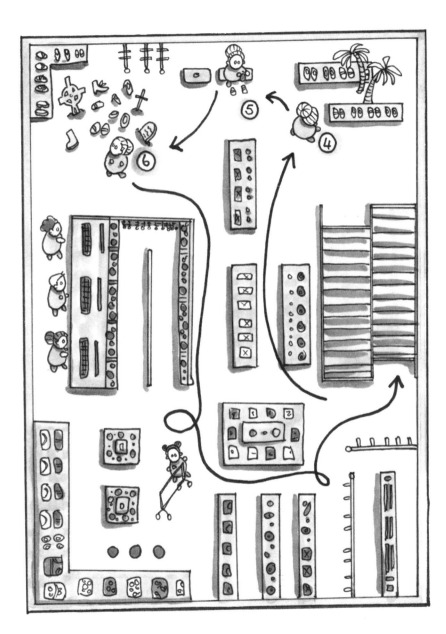

5. Try on a pair of glittery platforms that you don't need in the slightest. Totter about the shoe section, but avoid getting tangled in those ridiculous elastics that band the platforms together.

6. Okay, so you're buying the platforms. But first you must find your way out of the Graveyard of Abandoned Shoes. God, what a waste. But don't stop to grieve for them! There's no time to waste!

7. Get back down the escalator and pay a quick visit to Hosiery Hill. Pick up a pack of black tights, just in case.

8. Shite! Now your hands are critically full and you really do need a basket! Locate one, post haste!

9. Make your way through Handbag Alley without pausing to examine a beaded clutch bag. You don't need it! You didn't come to look for bags!

10. You've fallen victim to the delights of Jewellery Lane. Throw a pair of tassel earrings into your basket because they'd look great with that dress you got for Karen's wedding. And they're only €4. (You've a basket now! All is lost when you have to get a basket.)

11. What *did* you come here for again? You've got a T-shirt, tights, earrings, some shoes … Is there anything else you need? Nope? Best move on!

12. To the tills, where you encounter a discombobulating rush of buyer's remorse! Guiltily deposit the earrings where Purchases Go To Die (AKA the shelves of random crap beside the queue).

13. OK, time to pay for the rest. Very good. Now flee the store, taking care to bypass the pyjamas. Do NOT get sidetracked by the pyjamas this late in the game, girl.

14. Well done! You've made it through. But wait – didn't you go in specifically to get a tanning mitt?! Get back in there, soldier. Do not pass Go, do not collect €200.

GOAL:
TANNING
MITT

THE UGGS

Cast your mind back to the early 2000s, when the Celtic Tiger was roaring and Paris Hilton was the style icon *du jour*. What were you wearing? Ghastly tracksuit bottoms with something provocative and parent-horrifying – 'juicy' or 'babe', for example – written across the bum, I'll bet, plus an Abercrombie hoodie procured by some family member who went on a 'shopping trip' to New York. (People used to just 'pop over' to NYC for a weekend like it was no big deal. And everyone else would just nod and say, 'Oh you

were? How lovely. We're heading over to the apartment in Bulgaria next week', while bouncing on their trampolines and eating paninis.) And what was on your feet back then? Why, Uggs, of course – the most reviled shoe in the universe.

THE UGGS

You probably wouldn't be wearing the real Uggs because they were just glorified slippers, and you (or, indeed, your parents) would be damned if you were paying €100+ for slippers. No, unless you were rolling in it, the Penneys ones would do just fine.

Here, however, is an itemised list of reasons why the Penneys Uggs – and perhaps Uggs in general – did not do just fine:

- They were completely unsuitable for Irish weather. Just a few seconds outside would result in Soggy Sock City. If you accidentally stepped in a puddle it was game over. But this never seemed to be a good enough reason to stay away from them. (On a side note, why are raincoats and rubber boots never trendy in Ireland? Penneys should try to make over-the-knee galoshes hip. Or maybe they can do a range of embellished metallic fishing waders. These are all far more practical options than Uggs.)
- Exposure to the rain gave the sheepskin-effect material a really gorgeous pockmarked, grotty look. It was the kind of thing that made your mother clutch at her chest and wonder if you'd ever get any *nice* shoes. (You wouldn't, and you won't.)
- Something about these boots made people unable to pick

up their feet when they walked, choosing instead to do a sort of awkward shuffle. The memory of the 'swish, swish' sound of the soles dragging along the pavement is painful to me, even now.

- Those soles were made of foamy stuff – like slippers, because they were slippers – so even if it wasn't actively raining outside, the cold from the ground would seep up through to your feet. They couldn't even do what they were supposed to do, which was keep your feet warm! We should have just thrown in the towel at that stage, but we didn't.

- No, we just kept wearing them until one day, when you were hopping a gate into a muddy field or shivering in a GAA pitch dugout or doing whatever other grim teenage activities you did, the sole of one of them fell clean off. This was not an isolated incident. The soles had a habit of falling off at the slightest provocation. Great!

- Towards the end of a pair's lifetime, the heels would start to cave in, giving the wearer the appearance of having club feet. Which, as we all know, is something every fashionista wants to emulate.

THE UGGS

PLEASE...   ...LET US DIE

Bear in mind that all of these things would happen within the space of a couple of weeks. And what did we do when the boots eventually had to be written off, like an aul banger of a car? We just shrugged our shoulders and went back down to Penneys to buy a new pair, so the process could start all over again.

You'd think Irish women would have learned from these early mistakes, but we've never truly left Penneys Uggs behind. Each winter they call to us again from the shoe section, making us all sorts of promises we *know* they can't keep. Think about how cosy you'll feel, they seem to say. Imagine how warm your feet will be.

THANKS, PENNEYS

Remember the good times? When you first bought us and hadn't worn us outside yet? Remember how great that was, you know, before you stepped in that puddle and didn't take us off immediately and ended up with a cold that lasted two weeks? So fun. You got a few days off school, though, and we didn't hear any thanks for that. We're not complaining like, just saying. Come back to us. We still love you.

No, Uggs! It's time for your reign of terror to end. We deserve better. Never again shall Ugg-like boots touch our noble feeteens, ever.

EVER!

Except … maybe the actual slipper Uggs from the pyjama section can sit with us. We'll only wear them inside. Why are we so weak? God damn you, Penneys Uggs; we'll never be able to quit you!

76

THE LEGGINGS

It would be remiss to talk about Penneys Uggs without also mentioning Penneys leggings, which were the Zig to their Zag, the Ted to their Dougal, the Jed to their Ward. You know, they completed each other. You rarely saw those club-footed Ugg boots without a pair of black leggings rising up out of them.

Like the Uggs, the leggings are still an important element of Penneys' womenswear offerings and have remained basically unchanged since their first appearance. They are, to the untrained eye, perfectly fine – plain black material, stretchy waist,

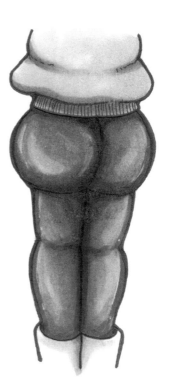

very comfy, cheap as chips at €5. They're often worn as pants (which bothers a certain group of people who should probably just suck it up at this stage), but that isn't the reason why they have achieved notoriety. No, we have one rather unintentional feature to thank for that.

Let me set the scene. You've put your new leggings on and are feeling all cute and casual, ready to go about your day. Nothing can bother you when you're dressed this comfortably, you think. Wrong. At some point, way too late to do anything about it, you catch a glimpse of your behind in a mirror and realise that your pink knickers are clearly visible through the deceptively transparent fabric. Gasp! How many people have seen your unmentionables today? Dozens? *Hundreds*? You spend the rest of your time in public pointlessly tugging your T-shirt down over your arse and standing with your back to a wall whenever possible, resolving never to wear the leggings again.

SURPRISE KNICKERS

THE LEGGINGS

Except you do, because due to some strange and evil magic you forget all about the leggings' treachery as soon as you take them off, only remembering their betrayal after you wear them again and see your *101 Dalmatians* undies reflected back at you in a shop window. It takes way too many of these incidents for you to at last relegate them to 'at home' leggings, but by then they've already made a knicker-flashing pervert out of you.

You'd think that after years of buying and wearing these leggings Irish women would have wised up. But that's not the case, it seems. You can still walk down any street in Ireland and glimpse more knickers than you would in the Penneys lingerie section. When will we learn? When will we *want* to learn? The fiver leggings are a false economy. We can do better, and we must. For the sake of the children, and also ourselves, and also the eyes of passing strangers.

But don't think that I'm telling you to never buy Penneys leggings again. No, I'm far too stingy for that. The velvet and/or fleece-lined ones they bring out every winter are the business, for example, and they won't reveal your orange thong to all and sundry. Just a little secret from one accidental knicker-flasher to another.

KNICKER FLASHER

A GRAND BIG PENNEYS

You could probably divide the people of Ireland into two distinct categories: the people who grew up with a Penneys in their town, and the people who did not. The former are the ones who could saunter in to pick up a neon tank top or a pack of 100 bobbins – or bobbles, or gogos, or whatever you're having yourself – whenever they pleased. They are the ones who likely spent many of their teenage Saturdays lounging somewhere near Penneys, making the grown-ups shuffling in and out of the store nervous. They are the ones who could make ridiculous teenage fashion mistakes willy-nilly without overstretching their pocket money. They didn't even know how lucky they were, with all of that right there on their doorsteps.

THANKS, PENNEYS

Or so would say the latter group, for whom Penneys was a kind of mythical land, like Tír na nÓg or Atlantis. Is it actually real? It couldn't be. People who had been there spoke of it with a kind of reverence, this place where you could buy T-shirts and hair clips and shoes for almost no money at all. Other kids coveted Abercrombie hoodies and Juicy Couture tracksuit bottoms, but you just wanted a real, genuine go around Penneys. When you actually got to visit it, you were overwhelmed by the breadth of *stuff*. And you wore your treasures with pride, proclaiming to everyone who enquired about them that they were 'Penneys, €2!' and basking in their envy. How lucky you were!

But there is a third, more complicated, category: the people who grew up without a Penneys until the wondrous day when one miraculously sprang up in their town, like the sudden appearance of an oasis in a barren desert. I know of this category because I myself am in it. After a childhood spent sneaking stolen moments in Penneys on visits to Dublin and Galway, we finally entered into a full-blown relationship when I was a teenager.

There has been no prouder day in the history of my hometown of Ballina, Co. Mayo, than when Penneys arrived on Pearse Street in 2007 (feel free to disagree, everyone else from Ballina). It had been the talk of the town for months – when it would be open, how many people they would hire, well so-and-so's daughter got a management position in there and SHE says, et cetera. There was a pile-up outside the door on opening day, like something you'd see at a flagship store on Oxford Street in London. And inside it was better than we could have ever imagined: all shiny and perfectly pristine, ready for us. There was an escalator! There were MULTIPLE ESCALATORS!

(As an aside: natives of small towns will know that the first arrival of an escalator into a store in the town is a huge deal. People would go into the anointed place just for the novelty of going up and down stairs without having to use their human legs.)

Most importantly – more important than the escalators, even – our Penneys was, at the time, bigger and better than the ones in Sligo and Castlebar. The biggest in the West! Take that, ye smug shites! (We were left red-faced a few years later when both of these stores were done up. Listen. Country life is fast-paced. One minute

you're at the top and everybody loves you, and the next you only have the third most modern Penneys in the West. But we carry on.)

What you need to understand is that a large, clean and well-stocked Penneys (henceforth known as a Grand Big Penneys) is a point of pride for a small-to-medium-sized Irish town. A Heaton's or a Shaw's (Almost Nationwide) is good. A swish new supermarket is definitely a boon. But a Grand Big Penneys? This is MAJOR. It doesn't matter what manner of dusty mother-of-the-bride boutiques and random soon-to-be abandoned vape shops make up the rest of the main street, a good Penneys marks you out as a key shopping destination to all in the surrounding area. It's a status symbol. People from smaller towns will flock to you, and you can be all, 'Oh yes, you poor creatures, come and avail of our beautiful Penneys. Please, no need to thank us; this is a gift from us humble yet still superior Penneys-havers to you backward and wretched souls.'

Like most things, however, it's not just about having the Penneys. It's about knowing that your Penneys is better than the rest of them. (Or at least the rest of the more rural stores. You'll leave the big boys in Galway, Cork and Dublin to their own devices.) If you're still wondering why this matters, you've obviously never lived in a small-to-medium-sized Irish town.

THANKS, PENNEYS

Let me explain. The rivalries between these places run deep, and the inhabitants will use just about anything to tip the scales in their favour. *Oh, so you've got a McDonald's? Well WE have two Supermac's, something we're going to swear blind is better than one McDonald's. TK Maxx is coming to your place, is it? Well, the government gave US a nice new road. No potholes on the way into our town, no sir! And sorry now, but our football team is better. We have two nightclubs. Your school uniforms are rotten.* The list of things to be compared and contrasted is long, but a Grand Big Penneys is somewhere at the top of it. And if the store in your town is cleaner, more spacious and better stocked than your rivals? Well then your town notches up a few more points in the never-ending game of 'Which Town Is The Best?', and everyone (in your town, at least) basks in a shared sense of smug satisfaction. Which is all we really want at the end of the day, isn't it?

WHICH TOWN IS BEST
CHECKLIST
☑ COFFEE SHOPS
☑ DOUGHNUTS
☑ DAYCENT PUB
☐ GRAND BIG PENNEYS?

You still might not think this is anything to shout about (you'll be a city mouse, then), but sometimes when I tell people I'm from Ballina, they say, 'Oh, I've been there. Ye've a grand big Penneys.' And I beam with pride. Yes. We do. And though this may not be the case any more, for a few glorious years, it was bigger *and* newer than the ones in Sligo and Castlebar.

IN PRAISE OF A RURAL PENNEYS

We've spoken about how important a Penneys can be to a small town. Beyond the rivalries and the comparisons and unofficial 'Which Town Is The Best?' competitions, however, there's something very special about a counthry (yes, I'm spelling it as you'd say it) Penneys that can't be replicated in the city.

I and a good portion of my friends from 'Down Home' always make a point to visit Penneys when we're in Mayo, even though we can go to one any day of the week up in Dublin. Really, I mentally pencil it in with all the other things I have to do at home, like Saturday: *visit Granny, buy stuff for the dinner with Mam, go to Penneys for a look*. It's very important! City folk might not understand it, but going to Penneys down the country is a completely different experience.

To begin by stating the obvious, it's *much* quieter, even on weekends. If you thought the words 'chill' and 'Penneys' could never exist in the same sentence, visit a store down the country:

it's always 10 a.m. on a Tuesday morning (AKA Prime Penneys Time in the city) there. You can take your time and browse at your leisure. Even if you've seen some of the stuff in other stores, you can take a closer look at it and maybe even – gasp – try it on without twenty people behind you fighting for ownership of a changing-room cubicle. The shoes are mostly on the shelves instead of in a puddle of heels and elastics on the floor. People are, like, smiling at each other. It's really weird. And glorious.

Occasionally you find things that you'd never find in a city Penneys, and it makes you feel like you've discovered something special (even though it's a blouse that you'll see ten other women wearing before the week is out). And here's the clincher: you can float from the accessories section to the homewares department without anyone getting in your way. See? Chill! And even when you're not at home, having vicarious access to a rural Penneys can be useful, as those of us who moved up to the big smoke from the country can ring our mams and ask them to scout out much-sought-after, sold-out items at home and secure them for us, if possible. This is expert-level Penneys shopping and a little luxury of which not everyone can avail.

Another nice thing is that a rural Penneys can be a bit of a community hub. It's a great place to go if you want to people-watch or quickly get up to speed on town gossip – so many excellent titbits of news have begun with 'So I was in Penneys and guess who I saw …?' There's about a 90 per cent chance of meeting someone you know, or at the very least of seeing someone you went to school with. Maybe you worked there at some point and still know a few people on the floor. Whatever it is, your standard trip to Home Penneys goes something like this:

Oh God, there's Jarlath buying jocks, good to see he's still knocking around the place. Is that Mr Moffatt, the Irish teacher? Hasn't he got AWFUL OLD. 'Hello, Mr Moffatt, hi, how are things? … Grand now, thanks.' *And ah, there's Michelle, who I used to sit beside in Fifth Year Maths … and a baby. Her baby? Michelle from Maths has a baby?!*

It's also the most likely place to be left standing with a friend of your parents, saying, 'Yeah, Dublin is great' or 'Yep, just working away in Molloy's', while they cluck and coo over how grown-up you are now. There's no chance of going into the Home Penneys without stopping to chat to someone for at least five minutes, so you have to factor time for that into the visit.

Despite all the benefits, one thing we rural Penneyites do love to complain about is that rural Penneys stores never 'get the good stuff' they do be getting up in the big smoke, which is a real and genuine concern that I wouldn't dare minimise for fear of angering my fellow countrypeople. But what we do get is space. Time. Maybe a little chat with an old friend you haven't seen for a while. And that's something very lovely indeed ... Except when you spot your teenage boyfriend and his new fiancée, and have to hide behind the fitted sheets to escape what's bound to be an awkward conversation. You could do without the stress of that, to be sure.

DODGY FASHION TRENDS OF RECENT HISTORY THAT WE CAN PROBABLY BLAME PENNEYS FOR

You may remember me saying that I envied people who grew up with Penneys in their towns from a young age, which meant that they had the ability to make teenage fashion mistakes cheaply. I stand by that statement, but I must also acknowledge that being bad at fashion does not suddenly stop when you turn twenty. In the past few years, we've all been taken in by some truly horrendous styles, which was made incredibly easy by Penneys being:

a.   extremely quick off the mark when it comes to detecting the latest trends, and

b.   having them cost about as much as a coffee.

And look, lads, no offence. We appreciate you bringing affordable fashion to the masses, but maybe you should start taking some responsibility for the missteps? We have previously discussed the Uggs and the leggings, which are of course the two totems of Dodgy Penneys Trends, but there are so many more to dissect. Here I will bring you five especially criminal offences to fashion that were recently propelled onto the streets of Ireland by Penneys. Give your cringe muscles a stretch there. You're going to need them.

#1: 'BOHO' HEADBANDS

First, we travel back in time to the mid-2000s, when 'boho chic' was *the* trend to copy. Celebrities like Sienna Miller and Mischa Barton off *The OC* were swanning around looking effortlessly cool in maxi dresses and fringed waistcoats, hippie headbands encircling their blonde lollipop heads. It was unfortunately quite difficult for anyone who wasn't Mischa Barton or Sienna Miller to pull off a head-to-toe boho look, but the headbands seemed like an easy way to channel the 'vibe'. Naturally, Penneys rushed to meet the demand, and for a very long time the hair accessories section was almost entirely made up of different types of elastic headbands. Some were thin coloured strips with no bells or whistles. Others had huge fabric flowers growing out of them. Some were simple, braided affairs, and still more were inlaid with diamantés and gemstones. Long story short, there were a lot of bleeding headbands and a lot of women wearing them.

They were supposed to be worn straight across the forehead with the aim of looking bohemian and ethereal, like a dainty woodland nymph that had just wandered in from the forest. The reality was that they'd slowly slip up your head, giving you a big poof of hair that resembled a mushroom. A mushroom that would later have a huge red welt across her forehead where the headband had been. (Mischa Barton didn't warn us about that, the wagon.) And for some reason, that was fashion.

EXPECTATION   REALITY

#2: FAKE HAIR

Are you really a true Irish woman if you haven't worn fake hair from Penneys? I'd argue that you aren't. Now, I don't believe they stock hair extensions any more (sob), but when they did, trying them out was almost a rite of passage – even if it was just sticking them on your head in the shop for a laugh, or a photo for your Bebo/My Space/Facebook account. The Irish female teenage experience went something like this: first shift, dabbling in Penneys fake hair, going to the debs, dabbling in some more Penneys fake hair, drinking cans in a field, and then dabbling in even more Penneys fake hair.

Nowadays, most of us are fully aware of what

good hair extensions should look like. There are people whose job it is to install and maintain people's fake hair, for God's sake! But we didn't have any of that back then. It didn't exist! So you bought what was essentially a quarter of a wig, stuck it haphazardly under your natural hair and headed happily on your way. If you fancied yourself an emo gal, you could get fake pink streaks and pretend your mam actually let you dye it. And if you wanted a funky bun but couldn't quite master the technique, there were (rather nightmarish sounding, now that we look back at it) scrunchies made of hair that would mimic the effect. Fun with fake hair for all the family!

Were the extensions an exact match for your hair colour? No, for they came in only three colours: blonde (yellow, actually), brown, or black. There was no nuance there. Did they resemble real hair in any capacity? No, for they had the weirdly shiny, knotty texture of bad wigs. But did they make us feel like a million dollars? Yes! Inexplicably and against all odds, that Penneys fake hair made us feel beautiful. Flammable, but beautiful. Even if we now want to burn all the evidence that we ever wore it, as well as every single one of those hair scrunchies, which sadly still pop up in store from time to time. They really should never have been allowed to exist.

#3: HAIR DONUTS

Look, those of us with long locks all need to employ a hun bun now and then to get our hair out of our faces. I would never slander the hun bun in its true state: messy, natural, maybe a bit greasy, but 100 per cent practical. It's a part of life! HOWEVER, the rise of Penneys hair donuts was truly terrifying to witness. 'What is a "hair donut"?' I hear you ask. 'Can I eat it?' You could if you really wanted to, I suppose, but it'd likely be best if you didn't. The hair donut is a round spongey-type thing that you wrap your hair around to form a bun. Sounds fairly innocuous, doesn't it?

The donuts actually started off quite modest in size and were rightly hailed as a handy way to get your hair into a polished-looking bun, a skill that had until then eluded most women. But as time went on they grew larger and sat higher on the head until women were basically walking around wearing circular hats made out of their own hair. Which sounds cool and avant-garde, but it really wasn't. The style reached its peak (or maybe its nadir? – it's up to you) in 2013 when Michaella McCollum was arrested in Peru sporting a particularly voluminous donut bun – perhaps the biggest one ever seen up until that point. She soon abandoned the look, as did everyone else, and most of us are already looking back at the donut trend in shame. A heady time for us all. Pun intended.

#4: QUESTIONABLE SLOGAN T-SHIRTS

This is the one thing the men's, women's and children's sections all have in common. Go to any store on any given day and you will find anywhere from two to 100 T-shirts with slogans of various levels of coherency. When I say 'coherency', I really mean exactly that, because Penneys T-shirts completely flout the conventions of English and form a language all of their own. Some just say things that would obviously be fine in any other country but are completely unacceptable here, like 'FRESH MICKEY'. (As in Mouse. It still wouldn't make amazing sense outside of Ireland, but look.) Some take such liberties with spelling and grammar that they would make even the most relaxed of pedants cry – possessive apostrophes are sprinkled generously here and there like fairy dust, for example, the infamous 'KISS THE BOY'S AND MAKE THEM SMILE' T-shirt. Kiss the boy's *what,* Penneys? In others, it seems as if somewhere deep in Penneys HQ there is a lottery wheel full of trendy buzzwords that they spin in order to come up with new T-shirt slogans. This is the only reasonable explanation for how we end up with tops that say stuff like 'SLAY BAE #SQUADGOALS IS WHAT A FEMINIST LOOKS LIKE *CRY LAUGHING EMOJI*'. (What?) Going through the store, you feel like asking the staff: why are all the T-shirts shouting at me? Why are these pieces of cloth so aggressive?

Take, for example, a top I saw in the women's section recently that said, 'I'm not in danger, I am the danger', like a very mild, textile-based version of *Breaking Bad*. I thought to myself, who is that T-shirt FOR? For what situation was it designed? I felt both threatened by it and worried for anyone who'd buy it (if indeed that ever happened), in case they actually did get in danger and a person came to help but then saw the T-shirt and said, 'Oh never mind.' It doesn't make sense! But we buy the T-shirts anyway because they're €4 and sure won't you just bring it on holidays to throw on and never mind that all your holiday photos will feature you with '100% My Type On Paper' (thanks, *Love Island*) emblazoned across your chest. In thirty years you'll look back and wonder what that was even a reference to and why you were so passionate about the saying that you had to have it on a T-shirt. And that's the evil genius behind Penneys' slogan T-shirts: they ultimately make you wonder whether you've ever really known yourself at all.

#5: MOCK SUSPENDER TIGHTS

Now, before I begin, I want to absolve Penneys of any real blame for the faux suspender tights craze. That blame should go to fashion designer Henry Holland, who created them for the hosiery brand

Pretty Polly – but his version was about €15, and you could hardly expect people who weren't Rihanna or Lily Allen (both early adopters of the trend) to spend €15 on a single pair of tights. Therefore, it was only when Penneys started stocking them that faux suspenders became accessible to the masses (not that we wore them to Mass or anything). And many of us bought them.

If you're wondering what I could possibly be talking about, let me try to describe them to you. Imagine a pair of black tights with a sheer panel starting at about mid-thigh and a fake suspender printed on it.

You see, Irish women have often grappled with the perceived difficulty of looking nice and/or sexy while also being warm. Do you go to the effort of doing tan and freeze, or wear tights and

LE SEXY
BIT

feel cosy but frumpy? It was and remains a pressing concern for us, so the advent of tights that combined the sexiness of suspenders with the warmth of tights was a revelation. On a typical night out in an Irish town in 2011 you might have seen ten to fifteen women wearing some form of faux suspenders, each feeling themselves to the max. And why shouldn't we? It's like we'd all beaten the system somehow. Take that, Irish weather! I'm warm and 'hot' at the same time!

However, Penneys had to take it all to a nightmarish new level, which was selling tights that *looked* like regular faux suspenders, except with Disney characters or Minions peeking out from above the knees. Suddenly, the dream was over. Faux suspenders had officially been ruined for us.

Did the mock suspenders ever really make sense? No, probably not. But then none of these dodgy fashion trends ever made a ton of sense.

CANDLE SCENTS THAT SHOULD BE AVAILABLE IN PENNEYS

Penneys could probably break even every year simply through selling candles. No trip to the store is really complete without spending at least five minutes wandering from shelf to shelf, unscrewing the top off each candle and giving it a good old sniff. We can't resist those little glass jars – mostly because they're €2 a pop, but also because buying one is a small investment in beauty. Your space, as cramped and grotty and messy as it might be, can smell nice. Purchasing one is a tiny act of kindness towards yourself. You don't have to spend actual thousands of euro on Diptyque or Jo Malone candles (someone who buys actual fancy candles may have to confirm this guesstimate; it certainly feels like they cost that much anyway). Penneys have even started to venture into Notions territory with the scents. Now you can find ones that smell like cardamom and mandarin and peach bellini and whatever you're having yourself. There is literally no need to have a €500 candle in your home – particularly as you'd likely be too afraid to light it ON ACCOUNT OF IT COSTING €500.

Penneys' candle range is already vast, but perhaps it's time for some new fragrances to be added to the range? Ones tailored to the real-life, day-to-day uses of these candles. I invite Penneys to consider all of these situations when whipping up their next batch. (Cut me a cheque later when these 'situational scents' are bestsellers, thanks!)

MAM'S MAKING A SURPRISE VISIT

Oh no! You just got a call from your mam. She's in the area, and she thought she'd pop by to see you. You'd love to see your mam and all, and she *has* promised to bring biscuits, but your place is a kip. What can you do to convince her that you don't spend your life in filth and squalor? Simply do a bit of light tidying up (i.e. throw it all in the cupboard under the stairs; sure it'll be grand) and light this

105

candle, which will neutralise her worries and fears and make you look like one put-together golden child. You're a disappointment no more!

THE BATHROOM CANDLE (SPECIFICALLY FOR BATHROOM SMELLS)

Quite simply, you put this candle in the bathroom and you never have to worry about embarrassing smells again. Spending some quality time on the pot? Strike a match and keep her lit. Having something spicy from the Indian takeaway? Light the candle in advance and enjoy some peace of mind. It's also perfect for new couples who are still in denial about each other's bodily functions. Keep that mystery going for a little longer!

UGH, IT SMELLS LIKE DINNER IN HERE

Some food smells permeate the whole house, don't they? You'd normally try to ignore it, but you have people coming over, and you don't want them to think that your house just smells like soup all the time or, worse, that you personally smell like soup. There couldn't be anything worse than that. Not to worry: fire up this baby, which will banish all smells of food and cooking so you can entertain your guests without fear of judgement. Not today, soup!

UGH, IT SMELLS LIKE BIN IN HERE

This features a scent that's very similar to the classic 'Ugh, It Smells Like Dinner In Here' candle, but it's even stronger — it'll fight that dirty-nappy stink that develops when you've been putting off taking out the bins. (God, that's an upsetting smell.) You still have to take the rubbish out though! This candle can't do everything.

THE HANGOVER HELPER

You know when you get up the morning after a Saturday night out? You go to the toilet or get some water and then return to your bedroom, only to be greeted by the assorted smells of your local pub: alcohol, cigarettes, body odour and a vague sense of shame. That doesn't make you feel any better, does it? But this candle will. Push all of your responsibilities from your mind and ignore the Sunday Fear growing in your chest. Strike a match, get a chicken-fillet roll, sit down on the couch and stick on Netflix. Let them soothe you.

THE ULTIMATE COMFORTING CANDLE

It somehow smells exactly like your mam's roast dinner. Take a big whiff – you can actually pick out the various elements of it, from the beef to the roast potatoes. Delicious, no? Just don't ask them how they did it. It's a state secret. (And probably illegal.)

MAMMY'S DIN-DINS

108

CHIPGATE

Before I get into things, I need to make sure: are you okay to go on? Because, no doubt, just seeing the words 'Chip' and 'gate' together has given you all sorts of flashbacks. That was a tough time for us all, wasn't it? We learned a lot of things about ourselves and the despicable things we'd do for a piece of Disney merchandise. But I'm ready to talk about it now, if you are. (Skip ahead to the next chapter if you're still not quite there.)

If you don't know what I'm on about, let me summarise: for a brief time in 2017, a sizeable number of people (read: way too many) in the UK and Ireland were driven mad by a cup. Not just any cup, but a cup shaped like the admittedly adorable Chip from Disney's *Beauty and the Beast*. 'Oh yes, the sweet if minor character that I've never really given much thought to before?' I hear you saying. Yes, him. In March 2017, to coincide with the release of the live-action version of the film, Penneys started selling actual Chip cups. And boy did it all kick off. Well, perhaps 'kick off' is an understatement.

For reasons no one has yet been able to satisfactorily explain, there was a huge run on these cups. They could not keep them in the shops. People who got their hands on one proudly posted about it on Facebook, leading to a sort of whisper network of shoppers sharing the names of stores where they were last seen in stock. Absolute chancers bought multiples and listed them on eBay for three times their €6 price, leading Penneys to place a quota on Chip cups purchased per person. A video taken at the Mary Street branch in Dublin shows a gaggle of customers circling a trolley like wolves, waiting for staff members to hand them a cup before they could even be put on the shelves. 'There's only one cup each today, sorry,' says a manager type as a cup is snatched from her hands. 'In five weeks' time we'll get more, all right?' I heard of no reports of actual fisticuffs occurring over Chip cups *à la* the French Nutella debacle of January 2018, but there had to have been times when it came very close.

In an attempt to appease those who didn't get Chip cups, and perhaps as a nod to how ridiculous the situation had become, Primark (ugh) in the UK released socks emblazoned with the slogan 'I wanted a Chip mug but all I got were these socks'. It was clever, but maybe too clever.

A collective cry of 'TOO SOON' went up from those who hadn't managed to get cups. The whole thing soon began to be referred to as 'Chipgate', the usual sign that something had graduated from being a Minor Kerfuffle to a Proper Scandal.

Then, as quickly as it had arrived, the mania ceased. People had clamoured for these cups, waiting and hoping and plotting and scheming for them, and then, when they had them, it was like, 'Great. Now I have a mug to go with all my other mugs.' Maybe there was some private soul-searching done about how it had all come to this, but for the most part #Chipgate was forgotten.

THANKS, PENNEYS

A couple of months ago, I found myself desperately longing for a very cute Harry Potter mug that was on sale in Penneys. (I love a cute mug! I'm only human!) However, thinking back to Chipgate, I never expected to get my hands on it. But, when I called in to my local Penneys, there were boxes upon boxes of them available. What had it been about Chip that got so many people riled up? We may never know.

I hope anthropologists of the distant future will study the videos and Facebook posts from #Chipgate in order to ascertain what life was like in 2017, in the heady early days of Trump and Brexit. And if one of them comes across a copy of this book and reads it hundreds of years in the future, I'll save them some time by giving them the answer: it was f**king mental.

NINE PENNEYS THINGS THAT CAN BE FOUND IN EVERY GAL'S BEDROOM

There comes a time in every person's life when they look at the place they are living and find it wanting. All of a sudden you have a fierce longing to repaint the living room or knock through a wall – to create a more open living space, y'know? – but you can't, because your landlord would sue you. Such is the fraught and challenging life of a renter.

THE HAPPY PLACE

Instead, you go to the Penneys homewares section, AKA your happy place, and search for the thing that will make your house feel like *yours*. Whatever the latest interiors trend on Instagram is, Penneys will have it on the shelves in double-quick time. (At the time of writing, it's succulent plants and chevron prints. They're *everywhere*.) Seeing it all laid out for you is kinda blissful, if you're twenty-seven going on forty-seven, like I am.

But listen. I've reached a place within myself where I am comfortable admitting that Penneys homewares stuff is basic as hell. Every gal in Ireland has probably gone in and lost the head over the same pineapple-shaped photo frame. It's so cute! It's *so* me, and apparently also *so*-that-girl-who-has-it-in-her-basket as well! But this is okay. Our collective love of trendy homewares unites us. The day we don't all have at least one of these items in our bedrooms will be a black day indeed.

BEDSHEETS PATTERNED WITH THE PRINT OF THE SEASON

When you first move into your own place – to go to college or start work or whatever your situation may be – Penneys bedsheets are par for the course. It's economical! A twenty-year-old doesn't have money to spend on fancy linens, nor would they want to spend it on bedclothes if they did. And that's perfectly understandable. They have Jägerbombs to buy.

As we get older, however, we split into two camps. There are the people who graduate to the Egyptian cotton, 400-thread-count world and the people who still don't understand why you'd pay

anything over €20 for a set of bedsheets. If you're in the latter, Penneys-going camp, you can enjoy a regular rotation of sheets in a variety of fashionable prints. That's what they mean when they say you should 'spice things up in the bedroom', right?

SOMETHING, BUT PREFERABLY EVERYTHING, IN ROSE GOLD

Name a household item and Penneys have probably done it in rose gold. Clocks, picture frames, toothbrush cups, cutlery ... yes, cutlery. You're still eating with stainless-steel forks and knives? Aw, bless you. That's cute. Rose gold (along with its cousin, copper) is catnip to the huns. I recently overheard one say that she'd have 'a rose-gold house' if she could. And I can't talk, really, because I have a rose-gold laundry basket. It's gorgeous and I love it as much as a human being could possibly love a laundry basket. See? I'm basic!

WHIMSICALLY-SHAPED FAIRY LIGHTS

Palm trees! Hearts! Flamingos! We are all powerless to the allure of fairy lights, especially when they're shaped like something adorable. Their faint glow can turn even the grimmest of rented rooms into an Instagram-friendly haven. One string, two strings, three strings, four. Drape them luxuriously all about your room for that Santa's grotto feel. Plus the dim lighting obscures the bit of black mould near the window. Sorted!

A BASKET FOR 'ORGANISING' YOUR TOILETRIES

'It will not do to have all my creams and lotions just sitting around like this,' you decide one day. 'I must find something to put them in so they will be organised and I'll know where everything is without having to go looking for it.' How nice that will feel! Cut to two weeks later when you're rummaging in the newly acquired basket, trying to find a serum that has been buried beneath receipts, hair grips, make-up and everything else you fired into the basket. But, as always, it's the thought of being organised that counts.

A CUSHION WITH A PUG OR A FRENCH BULLDOG ON IT

These are the trendy dogs. No other dogs are allowed on homewares, except maybe Yorkies. Even if you don't own a pug or a French bulldog, you will have something in your house with either of them on it. Most likely a cushion, from which the dog will gaze balefully out at you as you go about your day. His eyes follow you around the room, judging you and that half-full mug of mouldy tea that's been sitting on your bedside locker for several days now. He's not impressed, and you can hardly blame him in fairness.

A THROW (OR SEVERAL THROWS)

Because, if you hadn't gathered already, cosiness is key. This throw would ideally be one of those turbo fleecy ones that have a regular, patterned fleece on one side, then that super-cosy cream fleece on the other. I would go so far as to call these the Ultimate

Penneys Throws as they are superior in warmth and softness to every other Penneys throw – although I'm open to debate.

ONE OF THOSE POINTLESS LITTLE INSPIRATIONAL WALL-HANGING THINGS

These serve no purpose other than to remind you that you are in fact a unicorn. Or that you will accept Good Vibes Only. Or to do more of what makes you happy. Or you must begin the day with a smile. Or that this place in which you are standing is your HOME, because apparently we need a wall-hanging to remind us of this. But dammit if we love the stupid things anyway.

A LIGHT BOX/LETTER BOARD YOKE

A still fairly new but extremely popular addition to Penneys' homewares range, these boards come with little letters you can change around to form a message of your choosing. Click into any Penneys-related hashtag on Instagram and they can be seen beaming cutesy

communiqués into homes across Ireland. Did you realise it's only [insert number here] sleeps to Christmas? I didn't, before I saw approximately 200 pictures of these light boxes.

AND AT LEAST ONE EMPTY PENNEYS BAG

Always. You meant to throw it out ages ago (sorry Kevin!), but you might as well just start considering it a part of the decor now, like a feature wall. It's what Dermot Bannon would do.

INTERESTING DECOR, REALLY BRINGING THE OUTSIDE IN.

WHAT DO YOUR PENNEYS BEDSHEETS SAY ABOUT YOU?

A hot press stocked full of Penneys bedsheets is a rite of passage for every young Irish person (and some not-so-young Irish people – you can't put an age limit on low-price bedlinen). Even when you can afford some 'better quality' bedsheets, it's hard to tear yourself away from the sheer variety of colours and patterns that Penneys offers.

But did you realise that your choice of bedsheets says everything about you – your hopes, your dreams, your innermost fears and secrets? No? Because it really does. How you see yourself, how you want the world to see you: it's all in the duvet. Here's what can be learned with just a quick glance. (If you thought I wasn't above roasting someone over their bedsheets, you were sorely mistaken.)

MARBLE/PALM PRINT

Wow, #bedgoals achievement unlocked! You're slowly working up to total #roomgoals, but to complete that quest you will need to find five more rose-gold items (#allrosegoldeverything) plus some sort of faux-fur pillow (#pillowgoals). You are just two 'bare legs on the bed, holding a cup of tea and a book' photos away from reaching maximum Instagram likes potential and the most prestigious title of them all: #lifegoals! #GOALS!! (Not pictured: the time you ruined a set of sheets by spilling tea all over them while attempting one of those photos. That is so not #goals.)

DISNEY

… You're single, aren't you? I'm not being rude, it's just I genuinely don't think anybody in a relationship would or should have

cartoon linens. How could you look your partner in the eye? Even the strongest horn would wither and die when confronted with Winnie the Pooh sheets. In fact, it may be biologically impossible to have sex under them. This isn't scientifically proven, of course; I'm just confident that I'm right. The only excuse for a grown-up to have Disney bedsheets is if they are actually children magicked into their adult bodies, like Tom Hanks in *Big*. Love yourself! Buy less creepy linens.

HARRY POTTER

I'd nearly say the same about Harry Potter sheets as I would about Disney only the Harry Potter demographic is so overwhelmingly made up of twenty- and thirty-somethings that you'd probably find someone to bone you under the Marauder's Map no bother. It's worrying, but each to their own, I suppose? There's a lid for every pot. So instead, I will say, 'Everyone with Harry Potter sheets is a Hufflepuff.' (Oh yeah, I'm doing a 'Hufflepuff is the dud house' joke. Such a Gryffindor move.)

MERMAID/UNICORN

Aw, look at you. You're so quirky, you're so whimsical … and you *so* need a hefty dose of cop-on. You are not a mermaid nor are you a unicorn, despite what your duvet says – and the sooner both of these trends die, the better. Women deserve better options for bedding (and clothing, and make-up, and coffee drinks) than an endless parade of cutesy mythical creatures. What's next, centaurs? The Abominable Snowman? No! It's time to grow up. The real world is calling you, Linda! Answer the phone!

FLANNEL OR BRUSHED-COTTON SHEETS

You're one of those perennially cold people with skin so finely attuned to temperature that it cannot and will not suffer beneath regular cotton sheets. As well as the flannel sheets, you have one throw on the bed and at least three more strategically placed on the couch, in your car and at your desk at work. You don't care if everyone around you boils to death as long as you're at your ideal temperature. Your reign over the heating/air conditioning/bus windows could be described as dictatorial. People are afraid of you.

SHEETS FROM THE PENNEYS 'LUXURY' RANGE

Well, look at you! Aren't you all flash, flinging that extra fiver at sheets that are 'soft' with a 'thread count'. Harrumph. You probably have about thirty pillows on your bed, which you spend 15 minutes taking off each night and 15 minutes arranging just so every morning. Think of all that you could achieve in life if you didn't force yourself to do that. You could have a master's degree by now! And what's wrong with the lower-priced sheets, eh?

CHA CHING!!

€5

FONCY SHEETS
♡ ♡ ♡
So THEY ARE

You think you're better than the rest of us, deserve more than we do? We actually prefer our cardboard sheets. They're not scratchy, they're *exfoliating*!

PLAIN NAVY/BLACK/GREY

You are a single man and you haven't really thought about your bedsheets in years. These are legitimately the same ones you've had since college. Perhaps you should consider washing them more often, or maybe even throwing them away and getting some new ones? You don't even have to put much effort into that, just go back to Penneys and buy the exact same ones again. I can't help but wonder about the potential partners you might alienate with your crustiness, you see. But look, it's up to you!

A SATURDAY IN PENNEYS
(AS OBSERVED BY DAVID ATTENBOROUGH)

It's 8.30 a.m. on a Saturday morning and the local Penneys is slowly starting to come to life. Staff shuffle inside in dribs and drabs, wearing looks of trepidation along with their ill-fitting black slacks and shiny name tags. They've been here before. They know what lies ahead. Because, although all is quiet now, in just an hour or two this building will be abuzz with shoppers.

When the doors open, the first customers of the day amble in, savouring the order of the morning. These are the clever ones, who understand that arriving early will give them access to the store's best offerings. The racks of dresses are still arranged neatly according to size, the tables of knitwear and T-shirts are untouched. They are free to browse at their leisure, with no interruptions from their fellow shoppers. But this peaceful environment will not last for much longer.

THANKS, PENNEYS

Towards noon, more people arrive in search of inexpensive clothing, toiletries and smelly candles. In the women's section, we see two females approach a rail where only three black wrap dresses remain, the leavings of this morning's early birds. They eye each other suspiciously, knowing that they both need to outdo the other in order to win the prize: the final dress in a size 12. And look – one has indeed been faster, reaching the rack ahead of her rival and tearing through the few remaining dresses with vigour. Her speed, however, is no match for the brute force of her rival, who, with a brusque 'Sorry there now', shunts her aside. Stunned, the woman can only watch as the other woman snatches the last 12 from the rail. The defeated woman is left with both wounded pride and nothing to wear to Liam's work do tonight. She has learned, in the most difficult way possible, that there is no place for the timid in this unforgiving world.

At the main entrance, a mother with a large pushchair instantly experiences regret at leaving the con-fines of her home.

THANKS, PENNEYS

Shopping was once an enjoyable activity for this woman, but now, with her pair of younglings (Dylan, five, and Oscar, two) in tow, it is a feat of endurance. She needs to quickly source some polo shirts for Dylan's PE class. See how, with that goal in mind, she instinctively discerns the fastest route to the kids' section. It is truly incredible to watch.

The woman cannot afford to pause even for a moment to examine an embroidered jumper – without constant vigilance, little Dylan will run amok, upsetting piles of T-shirts and getting his sticky hands all over the faux-suede jackets. With ferocious intensity, she ploughs Oscar's buggy through the field of shoppers. Anyone in her path must move or be crushed. After securing the polo shirts and placating her squalling young with McFlurries, the woman will beat a hasty retreat back to the comfort of her couch and a nice cold glass of Pinot Grigio.

From the hours of 3 to 5 p.m., the situation in the store reaches critical mass. By a table that was once neatly stacked with T-shirts, a female employee assesses the damage of the afternoon. She's been in this section since 11 a.m., slowly building piles of tops that, like sandcastles, are swiftly destroyed by waves of oncoming customers. She quickly surmises that there is no shortcut that will set the table to rights with minimal work – she can only begin the

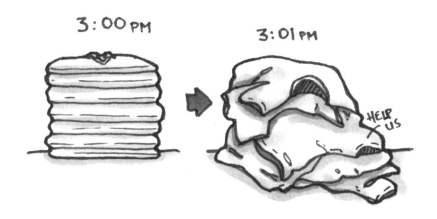

3:00 PM

3:01 PM

HELP US

mammoth task again. With a resigned shrug of her shoulders, she grabs the nearest garment and starts folding, stacking and rearranging. The table once again neat and tidy, she stands nearby, keeping a close watch on the result of her painstaking work. But look – a customer has spied the newly neat stack of pink tops and rifles through, pulling them out and sizing them up before carelessly tossing them aside. This process will be repeated several times over the course of the afternoon, leaving the young employee exhausted and despondent.

Deep inside the store, in the beauty department, gangs of teenage girls form an impenetrable barrier around the make-up counters. They snatch up testers, one attracting disgusted looks from fellow customers by smearing lipstick all over her mouth straight from the rather grubby tube. Another pokes her finger into a perfect pan of highlighter, leaving a sizeable dent. This is merely an act of marking their territory – neither has any intention of purchasing these items and now no other customer will want to. The girls chatter amongst themselves in what seems to be their own language, designed to puzzle the adults around them:

'I heard Zoella talking about this in her latest Favourites video.'

'Wow, looks so nice just from the swatch.'

'It's supposed to be a dupe for one of the Anastasia Glow Kits. And it's only €3!'

Researchers have been attempting for months to decode these messages, but no satisfactory translation has ever been reached. The language grows and changes at a speed that has never been seen before in any other species, with new words and phrases added weekly, even daily. There have been attempts to contact the girls directly for translation help, but all communication has been met with eye rolls and a torrent

of indecipherable slurs. It's safe to say that we may never truly understand what teenagers are saying to one other.

You might wonder where the males are during this frenzy. The store may look as if it is strictly the women's domain, but wait patiently and you *will* spot them. In some establishments small refuges with seats and phone chargers have been built to shelter the men from the fray. But here we can observe a few weathered males simply gathered in a corner, silently scrolling on their smartphone devices. All of them manage to convey an air of being dangerously out of their depth. One man has asserted his dominance over the others by claiming an abandoned kickstool as a seat. Every so often they glance up to ensure that their mates are still in their eyeline – but here we can see that one seems to have lost his partner. He performs the emergency ritual of standing on tiptoe to look over the crowds, jamming one finger in his ear and bellowing, 'WHAT?! I CAN'T HEAR YOU. I'M BY THE TIGHTS' into his telephone. The others ignore his plight.

Meanwhile, another male has wisely chosen to stay as close to his mate as possible, both for his own safety and to help her choose some decorations for their dwelling. As we learn from their conversation, however, the chaos that surrounds him has made him anxious and irritable and therefore not of much use to anyone:

'What do you think of these sheets?'

'… What? Sorry, yeah, they're grand.'

'But do you like them? I'm not sure. This pattern might not go with the cushions I got.'

'They're grand. Red is nice.'

'These aren't red, Stephen. They're raspberry.'

'… Right. Yeah, they're grand.'

From the puzzled Stephen in homewares we make our way to a forager in the men's section. From the panicked expression on his face we can determine that he had completely forgotten that it gets so busy on Saturdays and thus has timed his biannual search for socks'n'jocks *very* badly. However, he is making the best of a difficult situation, stuffing underpants into a shopping basket with dizzying efficiency. If he's lucky, he will zip through the tills and be

safely ensconced on the bus home within half an hour.

If he's unlucky, however, and there's a back-up at the tills, he will be forced to join the ever-growing number of shoppers huddled in the queues with their last purchases of the day. The scene calls to mind the evacuation of Dunkirk. One woman wears a look of the most extreme anguish; she's going to be dead late for pre-drinks if she isn't home and getting ready in the next half an hour. The girl behind her looks once more through the day's pickings, furtively discarding a top on a shelf. Yet another female will absolutely clatter the old dear behind her if she doesn't stop invading her personal space. A child wails somewhere in the far-off depths of the shop.

136

A SATURDAY IN PENNEYS

Eventually, with the shutters down and all shoppers cleared out, the staff begin the huge undertaking that is setting the store to rights: untangling and pairing up the piles of shoes scattered on the floor, filling the rails with fresh stock and fishing out all the disgusting rubbish people leave at random points in the queue for the tills. (Seriously, why do people do that?) When the job is done, they wearily begin the journey home. They, and the store, will now steal a few hours' respite, before readying themselves for the melee to begin again the very next day.

THE SIDE EFFECTS OF BEING A SEASONED PENNEYS SHOPPER

After careful research of the habits of regular Penneys shoppers, scientists* have observed that some of them come to display the same tics and traits. These symptoms are unusual in that they exist only within the confines of the shop and disappear immediately after the shopper leaves the premises. They're not painful and nor are they life-threatening, but they do cause some discomfort to the poor souls who find themselves afflicted. Here are the symptoms that have been identified so far, illustrated in this handy diagram.

a.   Vein throbbing prominently at the temple. This can only be described as being a result of 'pre-frustration' at the

---

*   By 'scientists' I mean me. Just me. (Note: I am not a scientist.)

noise and crowds that await them inside the store. This can often commence even before entering the shop.

b.   Jaw clenched, likely in grim determination to get in and out in 15 minutes without spending €20. This self-imposed pressure can worsen the symptom described in a.

c.   Eyes narrowed. This is done so as to determine whether the foundation stain on the neck of this top will come out in a wash, or if the size on the hanger matches the one on the label. The facial expression this produces has come to be known as the 'Penneys Scowl'.

d.   Neck and forehead become sweaty, most likely as a result of a and b. This can result in overheating if the shopper decides to try something on. Overheating, combined with ill-fitting items, often leads to a huge drop in morale, at which point the whole shopping expedition will be deemed 'a huge [expletive] waste of time'.

e.   Fingers of the right hand become twisted and mangled. This is with the effort of holding approximately thirteen items at the same time. Baskets are for eejits, after all, and sure you're not meant to be buying much, anyway.

f.   The left hand appears to have contracted some horrific skin disease – but no, it is just pockmarked with smears from lipstick and foundation testers.

g.   Legs tense, primed to outrun rolling racks of clothes, great hordes of students moving slowly (so slowly) through the women's section and bulldozer-like buggies.

h.   The feet also begin to throb. This is likely in sympathy with the head. Shoppers burdened with aching trotters just want to sit down, on anything really – the edge of a display will do, but the pouffes in the shoe section are the holy grail of rest.

If you've experienced any – or all – of these phenomena, know that you are not alone. There are thousands of us out here. Thousands!

PENNEYS' LAW

In late July or early August the rails begin to fill with cosy gear for autumn: puffy coats, bobble hats, ankle boots and, crucially, scarves. While in for a browse you spot one that's absolutely perfect. It's patterned with checks or plaid, made of the softest wool (or something approximating wool) and as big as a blanket. Ironically, you're actually looking for a swimsuit to wear to the beach on the one hot day you've been promised that summer, but they've all been cleared out to make way for the woollens. Even so, you're interested. This scarf would be ideal to spruce up your winter coat from last year. 'I'll buy it now,' you say to yourself conspiratorially. 'And save it for when it starts to get cold. Best not to leave it, because, as Mam always says, it won't be there when you're actually looking for it.' You walk back out of the shop into the 'Irish summer', dreaming of Saturday strolls in the crisp October air and feeling both stylish and sensible. It's an oddly satisfying combination.

PENNEYS' LAW

The weeks pass. That one hot day never materialises, so you don't miss the swimsuit. The weather becomes decidedly autumnal. Throwing a quick eye out the window one morning, you decide that it's finally time to bring out the scarf. You fix it snugly around your neck, feeling all sorts of smug over the fact that you bought it when you did. Then, on your way to work, you spot her. A woman, also with a vaguely smug look on her face, wearing your scarf. Puzzling. At lunchtime, another one, your scarf thrown jauntily over her shoulder. 'This means nothing. It's just a coincidence,' you tell yourself, willing it to be true.

Then, on the way home, there's one more, with your scarf pulled up over her head to shield her from a sudden spatter of rain. 'Ah feck.' The truth cannot be denied any longer. 'It's happening again.'

This is a phenomenon that has been haunting the women of Ireland for quite a few years now. We'll call it Penneys' Law. It goes like this: if there's something especially nice in store this season, you can expect to see every second woman wearing it.

(This statistic isn't official. I'm just going with what I *feel* it has to be, from experience.) The law can apply to anything. Pippa O'Connor wearing a Penneys blouse in an Instagram photo can inspire a mad rush on said blouse in store, to the extent that it's almost impossible to keep it in stock. And what happens when all those blouses are out in the wild? Exactly. Everywhere you look, you've got a doppelgänger or five.

PENNEYS' LAW

Penneys' Law keeps Irish women perpetually on their toes when it comes to sartorial matters. We all know never to wear something recently purchased from Penneys to an important event, for example. There is every chance that someone else will be wearing it too, and – horror of horrors – they could be looking better in it than you do. Even if the item was bought months ago and squirrelled away to be brought out at a later date, you just know that another woman put that same item in her wardrobe with the same idea in mind. It isn't worth the stress. Most people wouldn't worry so much about items for daily wear, but a Penneys' Law veteran I know has hidden all sorts of things away for an entire year, just so she could ensure no one else would be parading around town in them. She gets a little bit of satisfaction from informing someone that her coat was from 'Penneys, last year', with the 'so no, you can't get it' remaining unspoken. It's an extreme measure, I'll grant you that, but you can't help but admire her evil genius.

If I'm making it sound like we're all ready to leap at each other's throats over our unwillingly shared wardrobe, that's not completely true. While there is a little frisson of envy every time you see a woman pulling off your Penneys top with an elan you will never possess, occasionally two women wearing the same scarf will lock eyes and give each other a grim little nod or grin of solidarity. And, at times, having scarf twins all over town starts to feel fun. The sisterhood of the travelling Penneys checked blanket scarves, that's us.

GRAND PENNEYS TRADITION #2: TRYING ON SOMETHING IN THE MIDDLE OF THE SHOP

As children, we all experienced the unique embarrassment that was your mother forcing you to try on a coat or a jumper in the middle of a shop. You would stand there, immobile in a particularly puffy jacket, petrified that someone from school would come around the corner at any moment and witness your mam fussing away at the folded-up hood. Anne/Barry [insert the name of the meanest kid in your class here] would dine out on that image for weeks!

The long history of despair and discomfort in Penneys' changing rooms has perhaps understandably made people wary of trying stuff on in there. Most of us will just grab things we like the look of, check to see if they're the right size and buy them with the intention of trying them on in the comfort of our own homes – if they don't fit, we can just bring them back (or leave them to languish in their carrier bag with tags still on until we finally remember they're there, three months later). But sometimes, when the occasion calls for it, we will revisit that ancient method bestowed upon us by our mothers, and their mothers, and their mothers' mothers.

GRAND PENNEYS TRADITION #2: TRYING SOMETHING ON

We will set up in front of a mirror in the middle of the shop and have at it. Now, we wouldn't be stripping down to our underwear for all the world to see or anything like that. We do have a sense of decency, for God's sake. We're still Irish, when it comes down to it. We'll just discard our outer layers in order to try on a coat, or a jacket, or maybe a jumper if we're feeling particularly free and easy. (There have been reported sightings of women trying on bras over their clothes, but they are an anomaly. Also, I'd be very worried for their boobs if they were trying to judge the fit of a bra over another one. But I digress.)

Although everybody does it – go to any Penneys on any given day and you will still see mortified children being shoved bodily into jackets, or gals throwing on a cardi over their work gear – there's still a strange sense of unease surrounding the practice. That, I think, is down to the unique Irish fear of having people look at you. We are all for moving through the world without drawing undue attention our way, lest people assume that we only love ourselves (a great sin). The feeling of being watched, along with the general sweaty exercise of trying on clothes, means the average woman's inner monologue when trying on something publicly in Penneys goes something like this:

- ERRR...

It would be really foolish of me to just buy this jacket without trying it on, wouldn't it? I'd buy a dress or a top blindly but a jacket? That's just madness. I don't know what my logic is here but I am sure that it's infallible. But first, I need to find a nice, private mirror. I could just go to the fitting room and have a cubicle all to myself but why should I be going out of my way? I'm not made of time! I'm going to find my own personal corner of the shop floor and have at it. But what if I put my bag down and somebody steals it, or my other bits of shopping? Maybe somebody will walk away with my actual coat thinking it's for sale. I've heard of that happening and I'd be very upset if it happened to me. I guess I'll just hang my outer things on the side of this rail here. Close enough to grab if any shady coat-stealing type rocks up. And I'll stand astride my bags so no one will even think of trying anything. I look extremely stupid with my legs all akimbo like this, but at least nobody could accuse me of not being careful. But I don't feel right staring at myself in the mirror in front of everyone for so long. Let's just assess the fit of the jacket and keep things moving. No, look, everybody does this all the time, it's all right, sure as my mother says, 'Who would be looking at me?' Oh, that lady would be, apparently. Yes, here I am, trying on a jacket in the middle of Penneys. HAVE A GOOD GAWK. Does she think it looks bad? That must be why she's looking over. Psst, starey lady, is it very bad? It's best I know sooner rather than later. Actually, no, feck her. I look lovely in this. She's looking over at me because she's very jealous of me and wants the jacket for her own. Jesus, is it €35?! That's awful dear for Penneys. Things never used to be €35 here. But I guess I'll treat myself. Everyone needs a few good jackets, don't they, and I have some awful rags at home that need to be thrown out. Right, time to put all of my stuff back on and pick up the bags which are mercifully still safely ensconced between my legs and — Christ, it's roasting all of a sudden. I'm actually sweating. Did it get very warm in here? WHERE'S MY COAT? The feckers got me after all ... Oh no, there it is.

That sounds way more stressful than it should be, right? If we want this tradition to be passed on to the next generations of Penneys shoppers (and why wouldn't we? It's very useful), we need to get over ourselves. You must stand proudly in front of that mirror, your belongings scattered all around you, and put on that coat. Admire yourself in it. Wink at your reflection. Channel RuPaul coming down the *Drag Race* runway and do a little pose for whoever's watching. Treat Penneys like your personal dressing room. Own it.

THE TEMPLE OF TAN

The rise of Penneys as a proper fashion destination in the early 2000s coincided with Irish women's sudden hunger for fake tan. Well, maybe it wasn't that sudden – we'd always been extremely interested in getting a 'colour' – but until then this was only achievable by (a) boiling yourself on your hols or (b) doing the sunbeds. As much as we hated to admit it, neither of these things were very good for us, so fake tan was an absolute revelation. The wide availability of the stuff marked the first time it had been extremely easy to become the bronzed and beautiful woman you felt you were in your heart without setting yourself up for skin cancer. So with all that said, I should revise my earlier statement even further: we weren't just hungry for fake tan; we were *ravenous*. Tanning became almost a matter of public hygiene. If your skin wasn't a deep, rich cocoa at all times did you even care about your appearance? It was on the same level as shaving your legs or brushing your hair, maybe even brushing your teeth. One day we were all perfectly happy to potter around being pale and the next we couldn't so much as step outside without ensuring that we had a perfect California tan. Or at least the Irish version of a California tan: that is, streaky, patchy and various shades of orange. The desire for sunkissed skin has only intensified since then, though we're slightly better at coming out of it not looking like Oompa Loompas. But mastering that particular art did take quite a while.

At first there weren't very many options for the gal about town looking to give herself a completely different skin tone – you either paid handsomely for the tan brand of the moment, or you smothered yourself in Sally Hansen or Rimmel Sunshimmer, which inevitably went pockmarked in the rain and turned your hands a shade of purple seen more commonly on baboons' arses. I understand that this is an attractive trait in baboons, but it isn't exactly a cute look for humans. So what was a girl of limited means and a milk-bottle complexion to do? Why, go down to Penneys and avail of their finest tanning wipes, of course.

Yes, tanning wipes, the wicked items that were many

a young woman's first foray into painted-on tan. The concept was and still is completely baffling. Tan? In a wipe? You were sceptical about how well that could work, but you picked them up sneakily with plans to unveil the new, brown you at the next teen disco and watch as all the lads fell at your feet. However, your initial suspicions turned out to be correct. Use them without taking the utmost caution and you would turn out orange, streaky and STINKING of something that some people recognised as biscuits and others decided was curry. Not exactly parish-hall disco goddess material, but for €1.50 or thereabouts you'd make do. Anything to avoid revealing your mottled, ham-coloured Irish legs to the world. (I refuse to believe it's just me who suffers from ham-coloured legs. 'Ham' is the natural skin tone of most Irish people and it really can't be denied any longer. Where is the self-acceptance movement for ham skin? We demand acknowledgement! It could be called #hamazing, or … something better than that.)

But the days of the streaky tan wipes and purple hands are gone, mostly. Now we have *options.* Over the years Penneys have gradually upped their game to the point where they are almost single-handedly keeping Irish women in a luxurious, 'just back from St Tropez, darling' shade of mahogany. There's now even a Penneys brand of fake tan – which is miles better than their early attempts with the

wipes, thankfully – and they also stock Irish-owned companies like Cocoa Brown and Iconic Bronze. (The fact that Ireland has several homegrown tan brands says a lot.) While women might stay loyal to a certain tan for a while, they're always on an active search for something better, less stinky, and reminiscent of a colour that is actually seen in nature. And Penneys are always innovating in this field. Take, for instance, their recently released, curiously named 'tanning water' (a clear liquid that you spritz on and leave to develop into a subtle tan), which all who are in the know swear is the bee's knees. Seems sketchy, but we appreciate their dedication to eventually, some day far in the future, hitting on the winning formula.

All of these products are laid out in shrines to fake tan in every Penneys shop in Ireland – some even have an entire wall dedicated to tan and all the products associated with it. Because these days there is much more to fake tan than the actual tan itself. Take the tanning mitts, for example. You might think that there's only one type of tanning mitt, but there isn't. There are the bog-standard ones, yes, but there are also 'luxury' mitts and ones that go with certain brands of tan. There are also devices designed to help you tan your own back that are essentially sponges on sticks, doing away with the only remaining reason to have a boyfriend. There are teeny-tiny mitts designed specifically for applying it to your face. (Or you could divert to the sock section for fluffy socks for when you've tried everything else but still can't get the flawless application you desire – really, this works.) And we haven't even scratched the surface here in terms of tan paraphernalia. In these temples of tan you can also expect to see various oils and unguents that claim to speed up the tanning process and encourage a streak-free application. You can avail of a selection of shimmering body oils to put on top of said tan, with the aim of achieving legs as shiny as any female celebrity on *The Graham Norton Show*. (Once you notice all the shiny legs, you'll never be able to *not* notice them again.) Then, when you don't want to be tanned any more, there is a plethora of products specifically for scrubbing it off: exfoliators and wipes and scratchy gloves that will take away the scaly, greenish lizard skin that's the mark of a week-old tan. Do you see what I mean? There's just SO. MUCH. STUFF.

Don't think that just because Irish women aren't Day-Glo orange any more, they've left the fake tan behind. No sir. We've just gotten so much better at applying it. (Well, most of us have.) And the various temples of tan are a testament to that.

Long may they reign.

THE CEDARWOOD STATE OF YA

If you've made it this far, and you're a man, you're probably wondering how all of this stuff about jammies and scarves and knickers applies to you. Well, to be honest, it probably doesn't. Get ready to be blown away by this revelation: men and women appear to have different attitudes towards shopping. Women are happy to browse and try things on and admire wide-legged jumpsuits that we'd never buy, while in my experience most men would rather not. But hey, lots of women don't like clothes shopping either. It's often frustrating and sweaty and certainly an acquired taste.

As we've observed previously, many men take a passive role in Penneys, letting their mothers or friends or partners lead them hither and yon in search of whatever few bits they've come to get. But what happens when they venture in on their own? Do they ever even do that? Are they all secretly having fashion parades up there in the men's section and not letting us in on it? We couldn't be having that, so I found some men to ask. Yes, it was very difficult. Don't ask me to do it again.

So lads, what do ye be getting up to in the men's section?

Man 1: 'I would describe my relationship with Penneys as functional. If I need socks and jocks I'd go there. I'd generally be on the lookout for a handy shirt or T-shirt, so I could easily end up with some of Cedarwood State's finest. In my mind, Penneys is very much a box-ticking experience as opposed to actually going clothes shopping.'

Man 2: 'Yes, I'd also call it functional, for the most part. If I need a rake of socks or shorts before a holiday, I head in. I aim to be in and out in 15 minutes, if possible. If it's not too busy, I might wander to the homewares department and look for nice things, but rarely, as Penneys stresses me out.'

So no secret fashion shows (that they are willing to tell us

LAD SHOPPING LIST
☐ SOCKS
☐ JOCKS
☐ MORE SOCKS

about – I'm still not fully convinced), but it is interesting to note that the holiday smash'n'grab is an integral part of the lads' Penneys experience as well as the women's. Despite the practical approach to their visits, men still find themselves seduced by the other goods on display, just as we do:

Man 1: 'I'd also end up buying other stuff, though. Like, I went in for thermals once and came out with a hat, a scarf and a candle.'

The men may be all about speed and efficiency when it comes to shopping, but it seems there really is no one on earth who can control themselves around those Penneys candles.

See? We're not so different after all.

CHRISTMAS JUMPER LAD

There is a time of year when the men's section is alive with lads excitedly shopping not for necessities but for frivolous items. Yes, that might be hard to believe, but it's true.

"HMM."

"HOW STURDY IS SHE?"

HO HO HO

THANKS, PENNEYS

Not ten years ago Irish people would have openly scoffed at anyone wearing a Christmas jumper. They wouldn't have thought twice about it. Who do they think they are, like? *American*? We can't be having that. Not around here.

Not only have Christmas jumpers been fully embraced in the past few years, they've been fast-tracked to festive-tradition status. This has largely been facilitated by Penneys, of course, which stocks a range of Christmas jumpers that grows bigger and more elaborate each year. Go to the men's section at any point from September to December and you would be forgiven for believing that the only garments men are permitted to wear during this time are Christmas jumpers. There are racks and racks of them, one for every mood: tasteful ones and cartoony ones and rude ones and 'funny' ones and everything in between.

My God, the lads have taken to Christmas jumpers like you would never believe. Every December, roving packs of lads in Christmas jumpers can be seen on the streets of Ireland, merrily calling out to passers-by as they duck in and out of each of their twelve pubs. It's gotten to the stage where anyone who doesn't wear a Christmas jumper to their Twelve Pubs outing is thought of as a miserable Grinch, so they're omnipresent in cities and towns from the first weekend of December to the New Year.

CHRISTMAS JUMPER LAD

The various Christmas Jumper Lads in your local might just blend into one another at first, but look closer and you will see that not all of them are made equal. With a little bit of observation, you can easily identify the different types of Christmas Jumper Lad and the hazards they might pose to you and your pint.

A FEW PINTS AND I'LL HEAD OFF...

1. **Traditional Santy Lad:** Look, he's here, he has the jumper on like they asked, and he just wants to have a few pints and for everything to pass off fairly peacefully. He'll be the one glancing around, trying to check if the other punters are being disturbed by his mates' jig-acting. He will do you no harm.

2. **Punny Jumper Lad:** His jumper says something like 'Reinbeers', therefore he is the greatest living comedian.

He's thought up absolutely mortifying forfeits and rules for each of the twelve pubs, and any lad who doesn't do them is promptly labelled a 'dryshite'. He and Traditional Santy Lad are destined to have a falling out before the night is over; they only tolerate each other at the best of times anyway.

Punny Jumper Lad will likely knock into you and spill your pint while attempting some tomfoolery, and he will neither notice nor apologise.

3.   **Fair Isle Lad:** He put some degree of thought into how he could incorporate a Christmassy (but not too Christmassy) jumper into his usual 'look', which is skinny or slim-fit jeans, bare ankles and swoopy hair. He is constantly slagged by the other lads, but it's worth noting that he is the only one

of them who will still smell fragrantly of Hugo Boss six pubs in, when everyone else smells of Guinness and farts. (And Guinness farts, the most foul stench of them all.) Not the worst Christmas Jumper Lad to encounter by any stretch.

4. **Pop Culture Christmas Jumper Lad:** He means well, but he'll corner you to discuss (i.e. lecture you on) the latest big thing on Netflix, and you'll be looking over his shoulder at the craic going on behind him and you WON'T BE ABLE TO ESCAPE. In a busy pub at Christmas time, no one can hear you scream. These lads are fine in small doses, but make sure to have a good excuse ready for when you need to flee.

5. **'Bah Humbug' or similarly Scroogesque Jumper Lad:** He thinks he's too cool for all of this … but he's not. After years of being called a miserable prick for turning up without a Christmas jumper, he's gotten himself a little Scrooge McDuck number. That'll show them, he reckons. Entering into conversation with this lad will inevitably end with him trying to 'debate' you on something to do with politics or current affairs (he *loves* to play devil's advocate). Avoid at all costs.

HUMF!

⊗ BAH ⊗
HUMBUG

THANKS, PENNEYS

Of course, these are just the most commonly spotted Christmas Jumper Lads. There are many subcategories, and you can occasionally encounter a mixture of two or more of these examples in just the one lad. But there's no need to fear them – once you are able to identify and categorise these lads, your festive pub outings should go much more smoothly. Knowledge is power, after all, and your safeguard from all the worst types of Twelve Pubs banter. Use it well.

GRAND PENNEYS TRADITION #3: THE ANNUAL PRE-HOLIDAY SMASH'N'GRAB

Here's what's bound to be brand-new information for all the Irish people out there: Ireland doesn't usually have much in the way of a summer. There are one or two blissful days of sunshine when everyone goes stone mad, drinking cans outside and thoroughly sizzling their delicate Irish skin, and then … that's it. We don't see the need to purchase clothing specifically for those two days, so our 'summer wardrobes' are mainly what we wear all year round, minus black tights. It comes as no surprise then that when it's time to pack for holidays to sunnier climes we find ourselves in a bit of a pickle.

Do we have any flip-flops? No, as they are a fool's errand in Ireland, where the rain would make wearing them a squelchy nightmare. How about sun hats, fedoras, visors? Unlikely – unless you want everyone to think you're a gobshite. Shorts? We've never really had any need for them, unless you're one of those lads you see sporting them all year round, even in the middle of January. (What's all that about? Do these lads not feel the cold? But maybe that's a question for another time.)

Because of this critical lack of supplies for warm weather, before jetting off to Menorca or Tenerife or Marbella, we must

JANUARY SHORTS

EMERGENCY BIKINI BOTTOMS ↳

↗ EMERGENCY FAN

make our pilgrimage into town to obtain the necessary items. You'd think it would be a simple task, but panic and uncertainty turns the whole thing into a tropical-themed trolley dash. It doesn't really matter what it is or if you really need it – the fear of discovering that you should have brought a hand fan/bikini bag/third swimsuit when you're in Alicante and it's TOO LATE is enough to keep you filling up your basket. (When you're in this heightened emotional state, it's hard to remind yourself that they have shops over there too with all sorts of suitable gear.)

First things first: you're going to need a new suitcase, because your old one looks so bashed up and ugly now compared to the cute patterned ones they have in Penneys. You also have to get a pile of travel toiletry bottles that you'll inevitably waste gallons

of product trying to fill. Sunglasses are essential, but should you get two pairs in case you sit on one of them? You probably should, sometimes it seems like your arse is magnetically attracted to sunglasses. Next, you should pick up some kind of crocheted thing to throw on over your bikini for when you want to go to the poolside bar. It's objectively hideous, but glamorous holiday ladies always seem to be throwing crocheted things over their bikinis, so you may as well do that too. A one-piece swimsuit with strange cut-outs that would give you terrible tan/sunburn lines suddenly seems like a good idea. You'll worry about it later, when you have two triangular islands of 'colour' on your hips for the foreseeable future. And you couldn't be going without sandals, though you are forever making the fatal mistake of choosing them based on looks rather than which ones are least likely to cut your feet open. This cropped Metallica vest top is

undoubtedly crucial to the overall 'look' you're going for on this trip – you'd never wear it in your normal life but you have a feeling that Holiday You could rock it. Holiday You is of course much cooler and more effortless than normal you and wears off-the-shoulder sundresses without really worrying about what type of bra she'll put underneath it. Ooh, there's a reminder: you need to get some sort of heinous, flesh-coloured strapless bra for all these things. And a multipack of knickers because you don't want to be stuck for knickers. And some little pyjama shorts to sleep in, it does get awful hot at night so it does. *And* a huge straw beach bag to throw everything in, of course.

There, that's you sorted now. And how much? €108? Ha ha, that's nothing! All essentials for Holiday You! All things that will make total sense to you when you're packing the suitcase in a few days' time. And you're going to keep them for future holidays, so there's no way you'll be running around Penneys in a ginormous flap this time next year ...

THANKS, PENNEYS

Lies, lies, all lies. It might be time to accept that standing wild-eyed in a Penneys, making rash decisions about vest tops and sandals, is just part and parcel of going on your hols. In fact, I'd argue it's deeply embedded in the whole experience of being 'Irish abroad'. A holiday wouldn't truly be a holiday if you didn't spot at least three pasty lads wearing the same €6 floral board shorts every man in Ireland seems inexplicably drawn to. You'd be more surprised to arrive on a remote Thai island and NOT see a girl with the same beach bag as you, obtained in a similarly panicked fashion.

We can't allow these small acts of happenstance to die out. We must remain disorganised and uncertain. We must constantly wonder where that straw fedora we got before going to Greece last summer went, along with all the other summer gear we bought back then. (Seriously, where does it all go? Is there a black hole in each Irish house filled with vests and shorts? Is this a big Penneys conspiracy?) And we can ponder this until, once again, we must go, frenzied and perspiring, to undertake that tropical trolley dash.

HOLIDAY BLACK HOLE

ANCIENT PENNEYS PROVERBS

The Maximiser giveth, and the Maximiser taketh away.

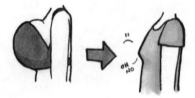

The early bird catches the fresh-off-the-truck Disney merchandise.

ANCIENT PENNEYS PROVERBS

Let she who has not worn see-through leggings cast the first stone.

It is always when you need a pair of black tights the most that the only size mediums left will be in navy and brown.

THANKS, PENNEYS

A reasonable pair of Penneys knickers in the hand is worth two in the pile.

Fortune favours those who aren't afraid to use their elbows.

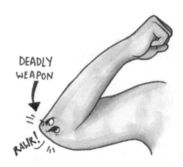

Fools and their money are soon parted by numerous 'accidental' €60 Penneys sprees.

THAT DAMN IRISH FLAG EMOJI

Allow me to describe to you a very modern heartbreak. You're scrolling through Instagram when you see a post from the Penneys/Primark page. It's a great page, actually – you don't even have to go in store any more to see what stuff they have in stock because they'll put up a picture (as will the surprising amount of #influencers who dedicate their time to documenting what is new and exciting in Penneys). It's *so* handy. You spot a gorgeous gingham dress that would be perfect for spring and make a note to keep an eye out for it the next time you're in the shop. No bother! You're all set! Except. EXCEPT.

You remember from your frequent visits to the Penneys page that with each photo they post they include a list of flag emojis to let customers know in which countries the items will be available. So you click to open up the full caption and eagerly scan the row of colourful flags within, sure that you will see the Irish flag among them. But no green, white and orange immediately jumps out at you. You look again, more carefully this time, just to be absolutely sure, and … no Irish tricolour.

CURSED EMOJI

— HOW ANNOYING

What follows could be compared to the stages of grief. At first you're in denial, because surely there must be some mistake. How can this beautiful dress be on sale in France, Italy, Spain, Portugal and the UK, but not in Ireland? It doesn't make any sense. We're right here across the border, so clearly it's a mistake and they'll stick the little Irish flag in as soon as they realise it. And now you're angry, because it's an absolute joke. Penneys was *born* here in Ireland, we are practically *related*, we knew them before they even called themselves 'Primark', for God's sake, and look at how they betray us. WAS IT FOR THIS? You're so close to actually commenting on the Instagram post like a saddo, that's how mad you are. Actually, you are a saddo, because you're suddenly really sad. Yes, no one has felt such sorrow as you do right now. You could picture yourself running through a field of wildflowers in that dress, not that you're aware of any fields of wildflowers in your immediate vicinity. But that's just the *feeling* you get from it.

The spectre of the Irish flag emoji haunts us every time we click 'read more' on a Penneys Instagram post. Its appearance or non-appearance is the thin line between joy and despair, a day made or a day ruined. We are grateful to you, Penneys, for catering to us lazy bums who want all the fun of the shops without having to go into town. But know this: you have now made us keenly aware of all that you keep from us. We are family, and you don't disrespect your family. We'll be watching you!

"HOW COULD THEY FORGET US?!"

THE ELEVEN TYPES OF PENNEYS SHOPPERS

By now, even the most casual of Penneys browsers will have recognised that the shop has some, erm, *idiosyncratic* customers. No matter where you go in Ireland, whether the Penneys is old or new, big or small, you will encounter some of these people in the aisles – the others you'll doubtless have come across in your own life. Some of them are benign, harmless creatures, others I would personally try to avoid whenever possible. But whether we like them or not, each one of them is deeply enmeshed in the fabric of the shop (so to speak), and a trip to Penneys wouldn't be the same without bumping into them.

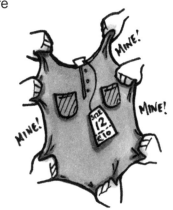

THE SHOPPER-DROPPERS

These people have absolutely no qualms about dropping every-thing they picked up in some random spot upon seeing that the queues for the till are too long for their liking. Nothing is good enough for them to line up for, not even a full basket of stuff they just had to have a mere twenty minutes earlier. They are the scourge of Penneys staff nationwide, who are left to scoop up the little piles of shopping they leave dotted around the place like sheep poo in a field. Yes, sheep poo in a field.

THE TUTTERS

The Tutters are the very close cousins of the Shopper-Droppers. They queue all right, but they want everyone to know that they're hating every second of it. Anyone standing near them will be treated to a full symphony of tuts and sighs – and if you're the unlucky sod who is standing in front of them, you'll feel them breathing down your neck, moving closer to you every time you try to reclaim some of your personal

TUT.

space. Incredibly, none of this makes the queue go any faster and only serves to make everyone tense and irritable. Who would have thought?

THE RED SIGN VULTURES

Is there a red-and-white 'Seasonal Reductions' sign on it? Then these shoppers are all over it, sorting through and seeing what they can nab for 50 cent. That top with the obscenely frilly sleeves no one else could find it in their hearts to care for? At €1 they'll see what they can do with it. That seemingly nice

dress with the nasty surprise of a back that gapes open to the bum crack? Stick a cami under it, it'll be grand. They are the ones lining up outside Penneys on St Stephen's Day for the sake of a bargain, even though Penneys don't strictly 'do' sales. You have to admire their dedication, even if you don't understand it.

THE TESTERS

The Testers are all over the make-up stands like a rash, which is ironic because a rash is exactly what they'll be getting if they carry on doing what they're doing. They're the ones you see brazenly breaking the seals on mascaras and liquid eyeliners to apply them right there in front of everybody, hygiene be damned. If they're particularly gross, they'll throw them back on top of the pile when they're finished with them, opening up the rest of us to a world of surprise eye infections (truly the worst type of surprise, next to surprise periods and surprise pregnancies). How can we trust any make-up product when there are Testers about? Ban them. Ban them all.

THE HEAD WRECKS

The Tutters and the Shopper-Droppers are not ideal customers, no, but at least they're not openly rude like these people. The Head Wrecks are the ones who corner staff members to give out about (a) the prices, (b) the quality of the stock, (c) the layout of the shop, (d) the mess that other customers have made, (e) the queues, (f) other staff members not smiling at them, (g) not being able to return something without a receipt, or (h) whatever else they want to get off their chest that day. They WILL be speaking to the manager. When a Head Wreck is in the shop, every other customer is automatically filled with crippling shame and wants to apologise on their behalf.

THE BULK BUYERS

These are the people you find standing at the till, silently watching as the cashier struggles to scan and bag €350 worth of shopping. They don't seem surprised or ashamed, which is hard for you to understand. What must it feel like, you wonder, to spend €350 in one go on anything that isn't car tax or, like, flights? They have to be either once-in-a-blue-moon shoppers going H*A*M or bloggers securing their latest #haul. There can be no other explanation.

THANKS, PENNEYS

No area of the shop has been exempt from their pillaging. They've got fitted sheets in there, some shoes, several bottles of shampoo, and a Santy costume for a dog. You can almost see the staff member wondering how many paper bags is too many. Is this one of those rare Big White Plastic Penneys Bags (AKA Super Kevin) situations? (All ex-staff members will know that the big white bags are reserved for especially heavy-duty shopping. Double bagging can only do so much.)

THE BITS'N'PIECES

You know those tiny Penneys baskets that seem a bit pointless? They were made for these folks. They don't come in to get anything in particular but end up filling a little basket with any random trinket that takes their fancy. Earrings, cotton pads, ankle socks, anything and everything from the little tubs next to the tills – if it's €2 and potentially useful, they'll try it. While the more sensible among us might balk at the idea of spending €20 with nothing much to show for it, for the Bits'n'Pieces it's almost therapeutic. Sure they're down a few euro, but how about this hair mask? It's got placenta in it! (Yes, for a time, Penneys was selling placenta-infused hair products. Don't ask.)

THE TREASURE HUNTERS

The Treasure Hunters are always immaculately dressed and put together, exuding a sort of rich-lady, only-shops-in-BT air that you'd think you could never replicate with stuff from the high street. But when you ask them where they got their gorgeous top from, they'll tell you it's Penneys. You find yourself doing that double-take that people still often do when they hear something lovely

is from Penneys. You've certainly never seen anything as nice in your local store, and even if you had you'd never have thought to wear it like they did. Sometimes, one person will embody both the Treasure Hunter and the Red Sign Vulture personas, making the cropped orange trousers you saw for €5 but dismissed as hideous look like Gucci. What is their secret? How will you get them to tell you? Blackmail? Coercion?

THE NEWBIES

This crowd is usually made up of tourists who have never seen a Penneys before but now would be quite happy to live in one, perhaps forever. You can almost see them thinking, 'Why did we spend so much time at the Leprechaun Museum when

we could have been here instead?' They wander around, awe-struck and jabbering at each other, gathering up everything that catches their eye before stopping to consider if they really have the space for a set of king-size bedsheets in their suitcase. Sure they can just buy another one for €30 (so cheap!) and check it in. It's fine!

THE PENNEYS SNOBS

A few different subcategories of Penneys snobs exist, and you've probably come across at least one of them. There are the ones who look down on people for wearing Secret Possessions or Cedarwood State jocks, as if everyone has the money for Calvin Klein. There are the people who reckon they're too good to be mucking in with all the common folk in the Saturday argy-bargy. And then there are the ones making loud pronouncements about the quality of Penneys' garments, as if paying €30 for a white T-shirt will protect it from eventually going yellow at the armpits. They're trying as hard as they can to harsh your buzz, but don't let them.

Despite this, each of them turns up at a Penneys from time to time, saying they just have to get stuff for the kids, or something for a fancy-dress party, or a few bits for a holiday – but they go to great pains to let everyone know that they would never come in here for anything else. Sure, Jan. We see you enjoying the bargains. Just climb down from your high horse and let it happen.

AND THE PENNEYS COMPLETISTS

They'd just get everything in there if they could. Wardrobe? 100 per cent Penneys. House? Decorated entirely by Penneys. Face? Created by Penneys. They're so inextricably linked to Penneys in the eyes of their friends and family that at least five people have bought them this book for Christmas. (Just a thought: it might behoove the company to start a matchmaking service at this stage, just so the Completists can get to say they found their husband or wife thanks to Penneys too. They can call it 'Penneys' Best'! A little money-making idea for you there, guys.)

PENNEYS
CHOKER

PENNEYS
PHONE
COVER

PENNEYS
BELT

PENNEYS
DRESS

PENNEYS
BAG

PENNEYS
TIGHTS

PENNEYS
PUMPS

THE SECRET THOUGHTS OF PENNEYS STAFF

It's an undeniable truth: Penneys staff do not get the respect they deserve. They're out there every day getting up close and personal with the worst types of human behaviour. They witness people turning into animals at the merest suggestion of a bargain, tearing the place apart for a pair of fluffy socks, then turning around and sniping about how the place looks like a bomb hit it. It's messy because you messed it up, fool! You're not the one who has to clean it up, either. But excuse me. That's just the former Penneys staff member coming out in me. If you've been in that position too, you'll know.

The next time you're doing something questionable in Penneys and wondering if the staff are judging you, let me tell you for certain: they are. Can you blame them for it, though? Sometimes it's the only thing getting them through the long days on the shop floor, folding and stacking and then folding and stacking again. Here's a small insight into the mind of a Penneys worker. (It's a bit more polite than what they'd be saying in their own minds, but you'll get the drift.)

- **When you're buying sexy lingerie:** 'Fair play to you, girl. Get your bit. Wait – is that him over there waiting for you? God, he's punching WELL above his weight. Maybe he has a great personality.'

GO GET YOUR BIT!

- **When you let something fall to the floor and leave it there:** 'Would you do that at home? No, wait, you definitely would, the state of you. Carry on, I guess.'

- **When you're buying something daft, like faux-fur sandals:** 'Oh hun. Oh my dear sweet summer child. You know you could wait two weeks and buy three pairs of these atrocities for a euro in the reduced section?'

- **When you ask us to check if there's any more in the back:** 'How do I explain to you that "the back" is a myth? Sure, it exists, but I cannot make sense of it. I'm going to get a sip of water and stand in the quiet for a second, though. Thanks for that.'

- **When you enquire after an item that was recently shared by a very popular influencer:** 'Looking for that? At 3 p.m. on a Saturday? Ha. Ha ha. Hahahahahahaaha hahahahahahahaha. I was almost killed by the stampede of customers coming in to get it at 8.30 a.m. this morning. But gold star for effort!'

- **When you've had second thoughts about an item and think you're being surreptitious about hanging it on a random hook:** 'I can see you, you know. You're not as sneaky as you think you are. I'm not mad at you for not trooping across the shop to put it back. Just very disappointed.'

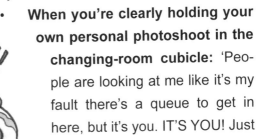

- **When something has no tag on it so you say 'Haha, must be free':** 'Does this smile accurately convey how much I would like the floor to open up and swallow you?'

- **When your child is roaring the place down:** 'This is all the contraception I will ever need. I wonder is there any way to convince head office to make all stores over-18s only. I think it would actually help business.'

- **When you ask us if we work here:** 'No, I just love wearing disgusting black slacks and a name tag AND a top that says "I Heart Penneys" in my spare time. Don't you think I look stylish?'

- **When you're clearly holding your own personal photoshoot in the changing-room cubicle:** 'People are looking at me like it's my fault there's a queue to get in here, but it's you. IT'S YOU! Just post it to Instagram and get out of my changing rooms, please.'

- **When you're buying something particularly nice:** 'How come I haven't seen this yet? Let me take a closer look under the pretence of folding it verrry carefully. It is absolutely scandalous that we aren't given first dibs on the good stuff. I should call the union over it.'

This might seem aggressive and unpleasant to you, but you have to understand that working in Penneys is an emotionally fraught experience. You can be staring daggers at a customer one minute and then, if the same person says or does something nice to you, feel like weeping the next. (Seriously, a lovely lady calling you 'sweetheart' can be enough to make you well up on a particularly tough Saturday.)

It's nothing personal! We just have a lot of feelings.

THE CHANGING ROOMS

So you've had a pretty successful Penneys trip, by all accounts. You've picked up some nice new tops, a skirt and a potentially lovely dress, though you aren't sure which size to get. Now you have a tough decision to make: do you shell out for the dress in two different sizes, knowing that you'll definitely have to come all the way back here to return the one that doesn't fit, or should you muster up the courage to try them on? Because courage is required. The changing rooms are seen as a lawless place – the Wild West of Penneys – where all sorts of weird stuff goes down.

This image has mostly been formed by whispers on the grapevine. Someone's aunt's friend's sister once discovered someone's rotten, discarded underwear, or somehow witnessed a woman try on a bikini with no knickers on. The most beloved tales, however, are much more vomit-inducing. Every person who has worked in Penneys has heard rumours of something shocking and vile happening in the changing rooms, usually involving some

sort of bodily excretion. If you were to take all of these rumours at face value, it would appear that there is a serial pooper leaving turds in Penneys' changing rooms all across the country. Because seriously, there is not one store in Ireland that does not have a changing-room poop story. As exciting as a case like this would be for the Gardaí (take a second to imagine them catching a serial pooper in the act and saying something cool like 'Cut the shite!'), it simply cannot be true. But the fact we're willing to believe that it is says it all.

Even if finding a poo lurking in a cubicle wasn't an ever-present fear, people would still think twice before heading to the changing rooms in Penneys. Yes, you can be queuing half the day to get to them on the weekends, but there's also the matter of your mental health to consider. It's universally agreed that the Penneys changing rooms are where your self-confidence goes to die. You might think that sounds overdramatic, but have you ever stood in front of one of those mirrors? They seem to magnify everything you've ever disliked about your body. Your belly is poochier, your legs are even shorter than you previously thought and you were actually incorrect about the number of chins you have – it's four, not two. Great! And you get to see all of that from the front, the side and the back at the same time, which is *such* a delicious treat, especially when you're trying on shorts or swimwear. I always wondered what my bra cutting into my back fat looked like! Thanks for filling me in, Penneys.

The mirrors are only Gretchen Wieners, though. The lighting is Regina George, the meanest of the Mean Girls. It tortures you and completely relishes every second of it. The harsh fluorescent beams bring every lump, bump and dimple into stark relief, throwing shadows under your eyes that make you look ninety years old. Who is this haggard, sweaty old crone before you, and why did she

"NOT THE LIGHT!"

believe she could pull off a denim playsuit? Even Rihanna would have a hard time conjuring up her famous swagger in there, and that's saying something. I've found that the best method of tackling the Penneys changing rooms is avoidance, but if that can't be done, maybe there's something to be said for getting zen on them. Look your mirror-self straight in the eye and say, *I know you're going to make me look like crap, Regina George lighting and Gretchen Wieners mirrors, and I don't care. For I am the Janis Ian of this situation.* Suck on that, bitches!

While Penneys' changing rooms are hardly a utopian paradise now, it's very important to note that they used to be worse. Much, much worse. Because not too long ago they were communal. I'll just let that sink in for a moment. When going to try stuff on in a Penneys of yore, you'd be confronted with a big room lined with mirrors, separated from the rest of the store by a curtain, where you were expected to suck it up and strip off in front of strangers. (There were separate rooms for men and women, which was maybe supposed to make everybody feel better. Cheers, lads.) It makes total sense, because, you know, the Irish are renowned for their totally progressive attitudes to nudity and complete lack of religiously induced shame, right? NOT. It was a nightmare made flesh, if you'll pardon the pun, and one that will take a few generations for us all to completely recover from. And I really meant it when I said 'not too long ago' – there is evidence that communal changing rooms were still operating in smaller, more rural branches of Penneys until 2013. Would you be well? You wouldn't.

So we should probably stop complaining about lighting and mirrors and be grateful that they let us have cubicles now. We'll never take those three walls and a curtain for granted ever again. Our self-esteem may be in rapid decline, but at least it's not happening on the public stage. We still have (the barest shreds of) our dignity.

OH GOD, EVERYTHING HURTS

THE CHECKOUT BITS

Many of the Penneys visits I have described so far in this book have been frenzied affairs where you barely even know what you're buying until you deposit the whole random mess at the till. But sometimes, *sometimes*, you are serious about only buying the one thing. So you find your tights or your shampoo or whatever it is you're after and queue up to buy it. That is all you are getting. Definitely. 100 per cent.

That is, as long as you don't fall prey to ... the checkout bits.

Each one of these eclectically selected items placed on the shelves near the tills is designed to tempt us. You're in the queue, feeling pretty good about your amazing willpower, confident that you've turned over a new, restrained leaf, when ... they get you. *Go on. It'll be fine. It's just three measly extra euros. That can't hurt, can it?*

So that's how you end up walking out with any of the following items: teeth-whitening kits, packets of Maoam sweets, deodorant, those shower pouffe yokes, the things you pop your bra in when you want to stick it in the washing machine, packs of three toothbrushes, antibacterial hand wipes, breath spray, protein bars, reusable coffee cups, body sprays that smell like an explosion in a sugar factory, tanning mitts, and cotton pads in various shapes and sizes. All of them are necessities of some kind, I suppose, but none

of them are things you particularly need right now. But you *might*. In the distant and unknowable *future*. And that's how they get you.

Because of this, queuing up to pay in Penneys can end up being quite an exhausting game of mental gymnastics. How many times will you pick up that packet of Haribo, put it back down and pick it up again? How long will it take your brain to decide that you actually came in intending to buy the Haribo all along? Not as long as you'd think. And no matter how often you remind yourself that it's all a fix, that the checkout bits are put there specifically to incite this kind of behaviour, you find yourself travelling down the same road again each time. *You really DO need another lip balm, actually.*

It's solid proof that we humans never learn. Ever. These days, I've learned to give myself €2 or €3 of padding on entering Penneys. If I come away from the checkouts with a two-pack of toothpaste or a mask that makes the dead skin on your feet shed like a snake (which is weirdly enjoyable), so be it. I won't fight it. At least I'll always have toothpaste.

PENNEYS AND EMIGRANTS

Here's the thing about Penneys: we slag it and act like it's literally hell on earth sometimes (and don't get me wrong, it can be), but we absolutely don't appreciate how good we have it.

At least, that's what Irish emigrants discover once they set up their new lives abroad. Where do you go in Toronto to get a tanning mitt? Is there anywhere in Beijing that sells nice, reasonably priced pyjamas? These are the things they don't tell you before you leave the country. I was absolutely disgusted on my J1 in Toronto when, assuming there would be a one-stop shop for cheap basic items like T-shirts and shorts, I ended up paying twice or three times what I would have done in Penneys. (Which I should have raided properly before I left. Lesson learned.)

Kate, a friend of mine who lived in San Francisco for two years, understands this completely. She quickly discovered that the United States, that great land of consumerism, was severely lacking when it came to places to get the few bits – she thought the chain department store Target would be close, but it was not nearly close enough.

'I found out that a three-pack of undies there could cost $15, and they were practically granny panties,' she told me. 'I nearly died without my Spongebob hipster knickers for €2.' (Haven't we all, in fairness?)

Penneys – or Primark, as we're now well aware it is known everywhere outside of Ireland – didn't exist in the US until 2015, when the company opened a massive store in Boston. Since then, eight more have sprung up, meaning a huge number of Americans are now experiencing for the first time all that I have described in this book. US YouTubers are doing Penneys 'hauls', filming their shopping trips and showing off the goodies they purchased afterwards, absolutely gobsmacked that it could be cheaper than H&M or Forever 21. Welcome to our world, lads! We've been living like extremely frugal kings this entire time and you hadn't even noticed.

THANKS, PENNEYS

One group of people you'd imagine who would be very grateful for Penneys' US takeover are Irish emigrants living on the east coast of America, where all the Primark stores are currently based. My sister, Emma, was one of those emigrants, and while living in New York she desperately missed the comforts of home – even something as simple as being able to pop into Penneys for a pair of tights.

She was sent regular care packages filled with stuff from Penneys – T-shirts, pyjamas, vest tops – just little bits that she needed. She remembers being particularly pleased with a bottle of make-up brush cleanser that you certainly wouldn't have gotten for $2 in a US pharmacy. On one occasion, though, she made a pilgrimage to the new Primark store in Connecticut, a good hour's drive from where she was living in the Bronx.

'It was overwhelmingly big, like *much* bigger than any of the stores at home. I got really excited when I went in, because it was my first time in a Penneys in about six months,' she told me. 'I bought tights, and a couple of other things that I needed, because I didn't know where I would get them for as cheap – while still being good quality – in the city.'

Tights seem to be a huge concern for Irish gals in the US – both Emma and Kate found that American hosiery simply did not live up to the high standards they had come to expect from their Penneys ones. 'Those 20-denier sheer tights. I could only find them in H&M, and they lasted about one wear,' said Kate. 'It just feels like the Penneys ones last longer and are still a few quid cheaper.'

Even if you're an Irish emigrant living in New York, which is close enough to a few of the new Primark stores, it's still not too easy to get your fix. The shop in Connecticut is a good drive away, as mentioned before – if you don't have a car, you could take a ferry to the one on Staten Island, but that's a day trip in itself. 'It would have taken me two and a half, maybe three hours to get out there,' said Emma. 'Like going from Ballina to Dublin.'

Imagine having to go from Ballina to Dublin just to get to a Penneys and buy a few pairs of tights! But perhaps it's worth it, when you consider the admiration the Yanks lavished on Kate's and Emma's 'expensive-looking' Penneys gear. 'Across the water I'd get compliments on things I was wearing, and I'd be like, "Ah no, it's just from Penneys." People would assume they were so expensive,' said Emma.

THANKS, PENNEYS

Kate and Emma had a few Penneys-related struggles, but they're probably doing grand compared to my friend Róisín, who seriously felt its absence while living in such far-flung locales as Vancouver and Ho Chi Minh City in Vietnam.

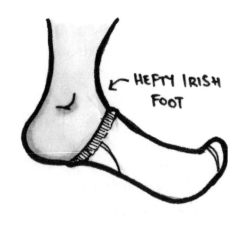

HEFTY IRISH FOOT

In Canada, she says, it was near impossible to find towels for less than astronomical prices. Towels! But the struggle got even more real in South-East Asia, where tracking down a pair of socks to fit what you would have thought of as standard-sized feet was a big effort.

'I miss those cute grabby hair clips and knickers that fit my Western-size ass,' she told me. 'I also miss the ability to run in and grab a plain T-shirt for €2 that you only need for one trip and know will get destroyed. I recently had to resort to buying a plain T-shirt in Zara that was four times the price you'd pay in Penneys, and it was only fit for the bin after a week of backpacking.'

So all you Penneys lovers out there – don't ever take it for granted!

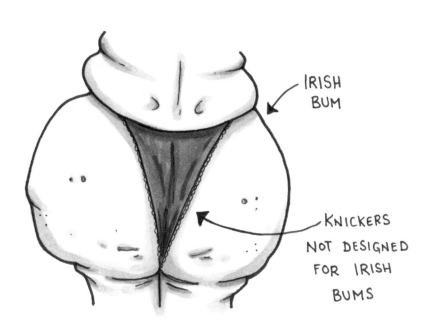

IRISH BUM

KNICKERS NOT DESIGNED FOR IRISH BUMS

THEY'LL BE THERE FOR YOU

Hearing Irish emigrants talk about searching high and low for plain tops and underwear when abroad in Penneys-less countries gives a chilling picture of a world without Penneys. I'm being hyperbolic, of course, but it's really quite difficult to imagine how everyone would go about the business of life if they couldn't rely on Penneys to cheaply provide them with the essentials.

You might scoff, but imagine the following situations:

1. Discovering a massive ladder in your tights halfway through the working day and not being able to pop into Penneys on your lunch break to get a new pair for the princely sum of €4.

2. Trying to break in new shoes and eventually reaching a point where it's too painful to continue on the bloody stumps that are now your feet but not knowing where you could possibly get some affordable replacement flats.

3. Realising that you haven't packed any knickers for your trip down home – it's happened to the best of us – and not being able to relax, knowing that you can't just get a multipack in the local Penneys.

4. Looking for a new 'jeans and a nice top' top at the very last minute and not just being able to barrel into Penneys and pick up something for €10.

5. Ditto trying to 'get the few bits'. Where would you go? NOBODY WOULD BE ABLE TO GET THE FEW BITS!

Well, maybe that's not completely true – the few bits could be acquired, but it wouldn't be easy. At this stage, you cannot deny that Penneys has made itself indispensable. It's always there for you. (As long as you get there before closing time. After that, you're on your own.)

There's probably no better example of this than the huge pop-up shop they set up at the Oxegen Music Festival in 2011 – it was stocked with everything you'd need, so no one would have to go without a sleeping bag or a rain mac or a flower crown (God forbid). And even without handy pop-ups on site, doing a festival *sans* a pre-festival trip to Penneys would be nigh-on impossible. Imagine forking out actual money for wellies you're only going to wear for three days before flinging them into the shed, never to be seen again? Perish the thought.

Whether you're a seasoned Penneys shopper or semi-regular browser, you can probably agree that it's saved your ass at least once. There's something about passing by and deciding 'Feck it, I'll go in for a look' that feels like such a treat, even if you don't actually purchase anything. And if you do spend €20 on little trinkets for yourself, well, that's a nice wee bonus. We'd all be a bit less glam, a bit less organised, a bit poorer without it. (But, thinking about it, maybe we'd be richer. All those €20s add up. I don't know – I didn't do Honours Maths.)

THEY'LL BE THERE FOR YOU

So yeah, thanks, Penneys! Thank you for the embarrassing underwear, the Saturday death wishes, the Chip cups, the questionable fashions and the absolute bargains. We couldn't do this thing called life without you.

ABOUT THE AUTHOR

Valerie Loftus is a journalist who was born and bred in Co. Mayo, though she has since defected to the Big Smoke. A graduate of DCU's BA in Journalism, you might have seen her work in *STELLAR* magazine, the *Irish Independent*, or DailyEdge.ie. Her personal favourite part of Penneys is the beauty section, where you will probably find her spending wild amounts of money on make-up under the pretence of 'getting the few bits'.

ABOUT THE ILLUSTRATOR

Ciara Kenny is a doodler from rural Kerry, which she refuses to leave due to a vague distrust of both motorised transport and townies. She draws regular cartoons for the Irish language site NOS.ie, and has contributed work to magazines, newspapers, websites and podcasts, as well as exhibiting in the Galway Cartoon Festival. She works under the name Ciaraíoch and can be found far too often on both Twitter and Instagram at @Ciaraioch.

FARE THEE WELL,
KEVIN,
OLD FRIEND.

MERCIER PRESS

We hope you enjoyed this book.

Since 1944, Mercier Press has published books that have been critically important to Irish life and culture. Books that dealt with subjects that informed readers about Irish scholars, Irish writers, Irish history and Ireland's rich heritage.

We believe in the importance of providing accessible histories and cultural books for all readers and all who are interested in Irish cultural life.

Our website is the best place to find out more information about Mercier, our books, authors, news and the best deals on a wide variety of books.

Sign up on our website to receive updates and special offers.

www.mercierpress.ie
www.facebook.com/mercier.press
www.twitter.com/irishpublisher

Mercier Press, Unit 3b, Oak House, Bessboro Rd, Blackrock, Cork, Ireland